Assaulted by Grief:
Finding God in the Broken Places

Carson-Newman College
School of Religion

Editors
David E. Crutchley
Gerald L. Borchert

Assaulted by Grief:
Finding God in the Broken Places

Carson-Newman College
School of Religion

Editors
David E. Crutchley
Gerald L. Borchert

Mossy Creek Press

ISBN: Softcover 978-1-936912-38-4

This book was printed in the United States of America.

Mossy Creek Press is affiliated with Carson-Newman College, Jefferson City, Tennessee. All profits from the sale of this book go to support student scholarships and Appalachian Outreach at Carson-Newman College.

To order additional copies of this book, contact:

Mossy Creek Press
1-423--475-7308
www.mossycreekpress.com

CONTENTS

IN MEMORIAM

Forgive my grief for one removed,
Thy creature whom I found so fair.
Alfred Lord Tennyson, “In Memoriam: A. H. H.”

Kym Blevins

1972 - 2004

Kristen Crutchley

1986 - 2009

Jake Ballard

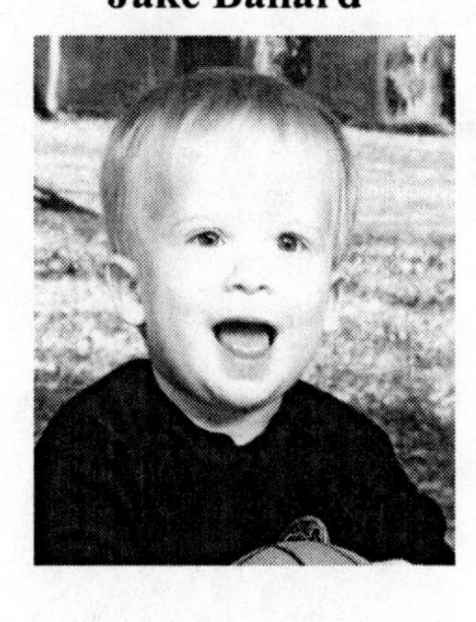

1998 - 2000

Aaron Garner

1979 - 1999

PREFACE

L. D. JOHNSON PREACHED THESE WORDS some years before the death of his daughter in a tragic car accident days before Christmas in 1962:

> *"Sorrow from the death of someone we love is like fire on crude ore—it burns with a terrible, devouring flame, but it proves what is there. Such sorrow brings out either our pitiful poverty of spirit or our deep resources"* (The Morning After Death, 137*)*.

Years later, he returned to the University of Exeter in England where his daughter had studied and wrote these poignant words:

> *Life is indeed a continual chorus of hellos and good-byes. Life would be richer if we could but remember that every person is a potential ally and giver-receiver. We must reach out and risk caring for one another, knowing that to care is to become vulnerable again, to give ourselves as hostages to time and circumstance. What we cherish we are always in danger of losing, and almost certainly must sooner or later relinquish. In a sense, every good-bye is an occasion of grief no matter how casual or temporary. Everyone who walks out of my life takes something, and I must be willing to have it so, for everyone who walks in brings something. Thus the balance between emptying and filling,*

> *impoverishment and enrichment, keeps being made over and over again.* (The Morning After Death, 63f.)

The purpose of this book, *Assaulted by Grief: Finding God in the Broken Places,* is simply to touch the messy world of grief. Grief is synonymous with profound loss and executes its reign in different corners of life's journey in different forms. The focus of the book is to stand in the valley of the shadow of death. Death is the incontrovertible fact and universal reality of life. To live is to die and to die is to leave those behind with a "shatteredness" and brokenness that stains the journey of life. Grief is the weight of loss and attacks all who stand in her path. Hence, the title that juxtaposes the "assault of grief" and the grace, hope, and mercy found on God's watch as we wander through the dark wasteland.

This book seeks to eavesdrop on those who have walked the trail of personal tears and lost their own flesh and blood through tragedy. It also offers a series of clinical pastoral responses to those assaulted by grief and a collection of theological possibilities drawn from the biblical texts that engage those who find themselves in the broken places or those who reach out to those floundering in the vortex of life's ultimate losses.

We are grateful and indebted to The Radio Bible Hour Inc. and Dr. Don Smith for their collaboration and financial support of this project. (The Radio Bible Hour Inc. is also the financial sponsor of the J. Harold Smith Center for Pastor Training linked to Carson-Newman College.) In addition, appreciation is expressed to all who helped make this project a reality. We write with a sense of frailty and humility for we have known from our colleagues and church families tears of grace and words of hope. Our faith resides in and is sustained by the Elder Brother who pioneered a bridge through the foreboding frontier of death. The cross stands empty as a monument to the love of God. The tomb stands empty as a monument to the power of God. In hope we reach out to touch the hem of the resurrected Lord's garment.

D. E. C. (Co-Editor)
Fall, 2011
Carson-Newman College

ABBREVIATIONS

ABBREVIATIONS FOR BIBLICAL BOOKS

Gen	Genesis
Exod	Exodus
Lev	Leviticus
Num	Numbers
Deut	Deuteronomy
Joshua	Josh
Judges	Judg
Ruth	Ruth
1, 2 Samuel	1, 2 Sam
1, 2 Kgs	1, 2, Kings
11, 2 Chr	1, 2 Chronicles
Ezra	Ezra
Neh	Nehemiah
Job	Job
Ps, Pss	Psalm(s)
Prov	Proverbs
Song	Ecclesiastes/Qoheleth/Song of Solomon
Isa	Isaiah
Jer	Jeremiah
lam	Lamentations
Ezek	Ezekiel
Dan	Daniel
Hos	Hosea
Joel	Joel
Amos	Amos
Obad	Obadiah
Jonah	Jonah
Mic	Micah
Nah	Nahum
Hab	Habakkuk
Zeph	Zephaniah
Hag	Haggai
Zech	Zechariah
Mal	Malachi

Matt	Matthew
Mark	Mark
Luke	Luke
John	John
Acts	Acts
Rom	Romans
1, 2 Cor	1, 2 Corinthians
Gal	Galatians
Eph	Ephesians
Phil	Philippians
Col	Colossians
1, 2 Thess	1, 2 Thessalonians
1, 2 Tim	1, 2 Timothy
Titus	Titus
Phlm	Philemon
Heb	Hebrews
Jas	James
1, 2 Pet	1, 2 Peter
1, 2, 3 John	1, 2, 3 John
Rev	Revelation

SOME MODERN TRANSLATIONS

KJV	King James Version
NIV	New International Version
NLT	New Living Translation
RSV	Revised Standard Version

Confessions of a Broken Heart: Jeremiah 20:7-18 as a Model of Spirituality[1]

David Crutchley, Ph. D., LLB.
Dean and Professor, School of Religion
Carson-Newman College

DR. LOUIS MCBURNEY, A PSYCHIATRIST from the Mayo Clinic, asks pointedly:

> *Did you ever feel that God had released you from bondage to sin only to leave you to die in the wilderness of the ministry? There are so many wanderers, men lost in a bewildering wasteland, no longer pilgrims on a journey, just bruised, confused, and hopeless strugglers.*[2]

This description is apt for the modern-day pastor who is buffeted and battered by adversity, crisis, depression, and the unrealistic expectations of his office. In support, H. B. London laments the "dehumanizing fatigue of faithfulness [that] becomes a way of life for too many pastors."[3] The modern prophet is not alone, for the spiritual giants of the Old Testament traditions wrestled under the dark cloud of despair during moments in their turbulent lives. Moses, wearied by the meaningless trek in the Sinai wilderness and incessant complaints of the rebellious Israelites, throws up his hands in desperation and cries "Enough—God be merciful—slay me!" (Num 11:14-15). Elijah's hour of power and triumph in the duel with the priests of Baal on Mount Carmel is followed by panic as the prophet scurries into the desert like a terrified rabbit. Unnerved by Jezebel's threats and his own self-doubt he requests death (1 Kgs 19:4). The mercurial Jonah, shattered by the success of his revival preaching to the Assyrians, pouts and with petulance calls for death (Jonah 4:1-3).

Yet the prophet from the backwater of Anathoth eclipses all of these others in his despair. Jeremiah is not known as the lamenting, weeping prophet without good cause. His diary, his intimate papers and his memoirs make provocative and poignant reading.[4] In these documents, drafted from the heart, Jeremiah tears away the veil and exposes the onerous burden of the prophetic ministry—the rawness of life as the servant of Yahweh.[5]

In these riveting self-disclosures we also witness the brokenness of human frailty and the vulnerability of the prophetic psyche. With brutal honesty Jeremiah discloses that he is a man stumbling in the shadows of the valley of despair. He is a "man under siege,"[6] and depression is his daily bread. Notwithstanding his reputation for melancholy, let us not forget that Jeremiah is no spiritual dwarf but the prophet cited most often by Jesus.[7]

The modern-day pastor finds an affinity with the weeping

prophet. We gravitate naturally toward these authentic cries from a broken heart as we seek answers to the problems of our own ministry and humanity.[8] The pace and toil of "servanting" can sap our strength. The pressures, weariness, and temptations of our task can erode confidence and obscure the clarity of our mission and purpose. As pastors we know that we are at risk and hunger for a spirituality that will sustain us and brace us in the field of battle. The tracks and tears of Jeremiah provide grist for our spiritual mill. The intention of this article is to reflect on the crisis point of Jeremiah's prophetic experience and derive principles for a meaningful construct of spirituality.

The Saga of Jeremiah's Pain

The prophet's nadir and spiritual doomsday is captured in 20:7-18.[9] Von Rad graphically writes that "night has now completely enveloped the prophet."[10] Assuming an historical link with the preceding verses, it seems like the straw that broke the prophet's back was the physical persecution meted out by Pashhur, the custodian of law and order in the temple.[11] He had Jeremiah flogged and placed in stocks at the Upper Gate of Benjamin in the temple. Bloodied and bruised, he is released the next morning and shares some choice words with his persecutor. It appears that Jeremiah holds himself together in the public eye, but alone with God subsequent to this traumatic experience, he becomes unglued and breaks down emotionally.

Jeremiah's pain is rooted in intense feelings of betrayal and "he complains of God to God."[12] "Overcome by his emotional fury," the Hebrew prophet "charges God with a premeditated deceit."[13] The two words "deceive" (*patah*) and "overpower" (*kazak*) used in juxtaposition call forth powerful imagery. The first refers to the seduction of a virgin and conjures up the idea of deception and alluring of consent (Exod. 22:16), whereas the second describes a forceful taking, a rape, and a violent overcoming.[14] A modern paraphrase would read: "How you sweet-talked me, and how strong you were."[15] Jeremiah claimed his will was overpowered and he was over-persuaded by God. This mismatch was a no-contest, for how can the human spirit prevail against divine coercion and compulsion?[16] What chance does a bantamweight have in the ring of life against a heavyweight!

The prophet's anguish resides in feelings that God has compelled his submission and then abandoned him. Jeremiah charges God during his discourse of despair with entrapment, and is "haunted by the thought that he might be no more than a plaything in the hands of an inscrutable God,"[17] a pawn expendable and disposable in the divine economy. For twenty years the prophet has thundered a message of doom and destruction with no results. Only the reality of *deus absconditus*—the hidden God—confronts him. If Jeremiah is to be the point man, at least God could support the message he placed in the prophet's mouth. The God who promised to underwrite the prophet's venture seems to be an absentee patron (1:19). Bright contends that "if Jeremiah had said in so many words, 'God, you have failed me,' he could have said no more."[18] The authenticity and credibility of the prophet is intimately related to the actualization of his message. There is none, and Jeremiah's consciousness reels with the recurring questions: "Why will God not engage the prophetic word and bring it to fruition? Why will God not clear the rubble and debris of ambiguity and clarify his intentions?" Divine passivity leaves the prophet in the lurch: integrity compromised and dignity wounded. Consequently, Jeremiah stands in the eyes of the nation among the ranks of the false prophets. His words are empty and earthed with no reality.

It was not the first time Jeremiah had lodged a complaint against God's recruiting tactics. In an earlier confession the prophet inquired: "Why is my pain unending and my wound grievous and incurable? Will you be to me like a deceptive brook, like a spring that fails?" (15:18). The prophet was claiming that Yahweh is an unreliable source like an unpredictable desert stream in a Negev wadi that sometimes runs with life-giving water and sometimes dries up completely.[19] The Hebrew prophet protests:

> *By comparison with the uncertain (lit. "unfaithful") waters, his pain is perpetual (nesah). What he is certain of is his awareness of himself; of the Other he has only a memory.*[20]

What has collapsed for Jeremiah is his trust in God's promised protection.[21] The specter of failure strangles the prophet's soul and an indictment of fraud is not an easy one to live with as the servant of God.

Accompanying Jeremiah's feelings of betrayal are those of bewilderment and helplessness (20:9). Again, Jeremiah is a casualty of divine pressure. He determines to remain silent and abdicate his prophetic function but God's word is like an irrepressible, raging fire that cannot be shut up in his bones. He is compelled to forthtell and foretell. The word is imprisoned within his soul yet it breaks out and speaks out with devastating consequences to the prophet. The prophet has two options and neither one works. When he speaks, Yahweh does not support him. When he is silent, Yahweh does not console him. He is cornered and each alternative guarantees misery. Richard Jacobson enunciates the prophetic paradox that guarantees failure:

> *His words will either come true or they will not. Should they come true, the prophet has failed to persuade the people to correct their behavior, and in their destruction lies his own. Thus his words may be true, but his cause is lost. Or else his words may not come true, in which case his mission is disqualified and his own status is in doubt.*[22]

Jeremiah's woundedness is exacerbated by the attacks on his self-esteem for he is disdained in the opinion of men (20:7-8, 10). The conflict and derision leveled at the prophet continues unabated. Jeremiah does not have the luxury of selecting his sermon texts: his messages of woe and impending calamity pit him against his countrymen—"whenever I speak I cry out proclaiming violence and destruction" (20:8). The burden of the prophet is that he must become a burden to his people, for prophets are never asked to proclaim what men and women desire to hear. Personal experience has taught us that hellfire and brimstone sermons are not easy to preach. Imagine preaching them for two decades!

The congregation of Judah was not sympathetic to such preaching, and it responded, not with repentance but hostility towards God's spokesman. Jeremiah's soul was bruised by repeated rejection. Of a sensitive temperament, the constant ridicule cut to the quick of his heart.[23] Derision, calumny, and rejection are hard to absorb at the best of times and Jeremiah's days yielded no release from such harsh treatment. No wonder the prophet's morale collapsed. The psychological warfare was endless. The backbiting and whispering campaign deliberately plagiarized a cliché from his sermons and Jeremiah's presence was met with the words "here comes ol' Magor-Missabib—ol' death and destruction!" The children taunted him, the women gossiped about him, and the men in the marketplace scoffed and baited him. The populace of Judah caricatured him as a demented and deluded messenger crying "wolf!" Such ridicule chafed the chords of his heart. In the midst of his words of fire there was a river of tears. His life as a prophet was "an unbroken series of torments"[24] and the "dark shadow of failure seemed to blight his life."[25]

Where does the prophet find relief or an ally? God has deserted him. His so-called friends watch expectantly for a false step that will bring him down (20:10). Jeremiah is in every way "a man of intensive dispute,"[26] at odds with the royal apparatus, his prophetic counterparts, and even his own kith and kin from Anathoth. The prophet discovers the reality that a man of his office has no honor in his own town. Probably embarrassed by Jeremiah's attack on traditional Judean theology, namely that Jerusalem and its temple were inviolate, his own community plotted to assassinate him (11:18-23).[27] The conspiracy against Jeremiah is rebellion against God because the prophet stands and speaks in the sandals of God. Jeremiah stands alone, because even the solace of a life partner has been denied him (16:1-4).[28] Blackmailed by God, blackballed by his family, the messenger of God is a "victim of heaven and earth."[29] Walther Zimmerli claims that "the human persecutor is not the only enemy."[30] Davidson continues to bring out the prophet's isolation and utter alienation: "You do not openly attack the temple and get invited to the Jerusalem priest's fraternal, you do not walk through the streets of Jerusalem advocating destruction and then go for a drink in the officer's mess."[31]

At heart Jeremiah was a patriot, and to be charged with treason when on a redemptive mission was a bitter pill to swallow. As Heschel states of his double mediation: "He was a person overwhelmed by sympathy for God and sympathy for man. Standing before the people he pleaded for God; standing before God he pleaded for his people."[32] The message of God's covenant-faithfulness fell on the deaf ears of a fickle people and Jeremiah experienced the pain of unrequited love. Polarized, an outcast living as a leper in a wilderness of rejection, the prophet bore faithfully the emotional and physical stigmata of his office. As Brueggemann aptly remarks, "the vocation of the prophet is a conflicted way to live" and "dispute is definitional to his call."[33]

The emotional turbulence of the prophet reaches its depths in the *cri d'coeur* of 20:14-18.[34] For here the prophet staggered into the deepest abyss, and total disillusionment is written across his self-curse. In this pit he wrote a poem of violent rejection and self-hatred. To curse God was a capital offence, so the prophet promptly curses the day of his birth. To curse one's father was a crime worthy of death by stoning, so Jeremiah slams an imprecation at the messenger carrying the joyous news of his birth to his father. The father's joy contrasts the tortured angst of Jeremiah's soul. He yearns with a before-birth death wish that his mother's womb had become his grave (20:17-18). The prophet's concluding cry of dereliction, "Why was I ever born!" reflects the depths of his emotional trauma and disintegration.[35] The prophet is on the cross!

Implications of Pain in Ministry

Have you ever walked where Jeremiah trod—down the *via dolorosa* because of your commitment to a ministerial vocation? Are you currently experiencing the crisis of self-doubt and disillusionment in ministry? What lessons and principles can we glean from Jeremiah's pilgrimage of sorrow that will enable us to construct a theology of spirituality in similar straits?

Facing the tension: frankness and frustration, blatant honesty and suppression.

The first principle derived from this Jeremianic saga is that we need the courage to formulate our doubts. This calls for honest-to-God frankness and blatant honesty. Jeremiah's confessions stun us with their fearless candor. Yet they are not the tantrums of a troubled toddler, nor the exclamations of an impetuous adolescent, but they are the cries from a bleeding pastor's heart.

Has each one of us in ministry not felt at times in the corridors of our heart's frustration, anger, and bitterness at the course our life has taken? We have placed our lives on the line and the pay-back has been pain, hurt, and conflict. Our families have not escaped unscathed and ministry has exacted a heavy toll. We expected divine compensation for mortgaging our own desires, dreams, and aspirations. At least we anticipated that obedience to the divine call meant that God would ensure our acceptance by his people and that he would go ahead of us and prepare a comfortable way. Instead our church backyard is a battleground, a conflict zone where the scars of conflict have become acute disappointment, stress, and, dare we say it, disillusionment. At times we have been left numb with the futility of our task and left wondering if this Christianity we espouse is for real, or a ruse, a charade, a hollow game.

Bernhard Anderson argues, however, for guardedness in our expostulations:

> *Few individuals have suffered as deeply, and we must be careful not to criticize too easily the passionate queries and protests that Jeremiah hurled at God. Yet his prayers–like so many human utterances–express the self-pity and even the self-righteousness that often arises when a person's faith is put to the severest test. His question, 'Why does this happen to me?' suggests that he had been badly treated after all the sacrifices he had made for Yahweh's sake.*[36]

Robert Davidson provides a helpful counterbalance to Anderson's words:

> *In such prayers we find the same kind of raw honesty which we noted in the psalms of lament, an honesty intensified by a sharply personal edge which we can relate to conflict situations in the prophet's life. If we find the honesty too raw, in some of its expressions, particularly in the prayers for vengeance, let us remember two things:*
>
> *(a) It is not easy for those of us who live carefully in the shallows to enter sympathetically into hurt cries which come to us from the depths.*
>
> *(b) It was of no little importance that Jeremiah, following the psalms of lament, shaped that totality of his experience into prayers. He might otherwise have ceased to pray, or have so carefully shaped his prayers that they expressed only a pseudo piety which would have hurt no one but himself.*[37]

Note that this "confessing, complaining prayer"[38] hurls his fundamental questions heavenward. That his complaints and laments are addressed to God is salutary. He does not talk behind God's back. In the same way, let us resolve not to unnerve and unsettle our congregations and students with "blasphemous" thoughts and volatile feelings. Let us deposit our doubts and fears at the door of God and our hearts at his feet. The prophet does not opt for the traditional model of piety, namely, a suppression of feelings and doubts. In fact, the messenger of God was enabled to maintain his sanity because "he did not hesitate to give vent to his feelings of despair and bitterness."[39] Jeremiah's doubts and protests carry him to God and not away from him.[40] Vangemeren comments wisely that "in the tension of suffering and submission to God's freedom, the godly focus their hope in God alone."[41]

James Ward reminds us unequivocally that "the alternative to fearless honesty is fearful dishonesty."[42] Jeremiah plumbs the depths of honesty in his "heated" dialogue with God that "at times trod perilously close to blasphemy."[43] This servant of God can never be accused of timidity in the prayer cellar. There are prettier and more reverent prayers in history, as Thomas-a-Kempis' *The Imitation of Christ* will attest, but there are few prayers prayed with such fervor, honesty, and urgency. Jeremiah is not a man rationally sequencing his soliloquy but a prophet pouring out his whole self in impetuous outbursts before his God. Eugene Peterson, noted exponent on spiritual formation, argues that our "anger can be a measure of our faith" and "believers argue with God, skeptics with each other."[44] Joel Gregory adds that "telling God how you feel won't make Him so dizzy He falls off his throne. He's taken on bigger and harder prayers than ours."[45]

Our prayers are an opportunity to voice the mood of our soul—dialogue with God initiated for the purpose of laying before him "praise and thanksgiving, petition and intercession, lament and complaint."[46] They articulate our faith and life-story with God. Timothy Polk points to the "self-constituting quality" of prayer: "In the effort to gather one's life and present it before God, the self is being explored, expressed, shaped and reshaped."[47] Prayers are in essence flutters of faith from our heart that God can work things out. The very posture of prayer implies an overture of confidence in God. The prayers of the servant of God leave the onus and responsibility where it belongs: on the divine shoulders.

Experiencing the silence of God

A second lesson to be drawn from Jeremiah chapter 20 is that we need the courage to accept the reality of God's silence. The prophet looks toward God, tears in the heart, and beats on heaven's brass doors with bleeding knuckles. The silence of God seems deafening and Jeremiah accuses God of closing up shop and leaving town. What happens when we reach a point in our ministry of going through the motions when what we have been most confidently preaching or teaching about the reality of God no longer makes sense in our experience? Do we walk from the pulpit or the classroom lectern into the night never to return? We have to trudge painstakingly through the dark night of our soul. The premise behind grace is mystery and we cling to the belief that God is at the helm of life as we negotiate the doldrums and the treacherous rocks of forsakenness and despair. Von Rad's reminder is timely that "if God brought the life of the most faithful of his ambassadors into so terrible and utterly uncomprehended a night and there to all appearances allowed him to come to utter grief, this remains God's secret."[48]

Such an experience must have been the case for a black pastor living in apartheid South Africa. How he must have found the confessions of Jeremiah providing anguished points of contact and emotional solidarity. For that pastor and his people who suffered the onslaught of oppressive racist policies and even the deep emotional and psychological wounds articulated by the late Steve Biko,[49] the silence of God must have seemed interminable. During these centuries of exploitation the prayers offered up for peace, equity, and justice must have appeared hollow rhetoric taking no root in the divine purpose.

Yet Jeremiah was not the Old Testament Nietzsche.[50] At the point of deepest gloom the prophet turns "toward the transcendent" and "discovers profound new meaning and recognizes God's salvific presence."[51] "In prayer God is not merely audience, he is partner," writes Peterson, "Jeremiah has spoken honestly, now he listens expectantly."[52] Prayer stills our hearts for often we enter the prayer tryst confused and come out confident. More than likely our present crisis and dire circumstances remain unchanged but prayer enables us to view the world and our situation with God's eyes. It helps us to abandon our rational muddle and yield to divine providence. For the "assumption that 'response' is integral to prayer, or that prayer is somehow incomplete if there is no response" is illegitimate.[53]

The silence of God resonates with meaning and amidst uncertainty the prophet projects an incipient faith –"the Lord is with me like a mighty warrior" (20:11). Nevertheless, God's presence is elusive and the divine demolishes our suspect patterns of predictability. For the God who reveals himself is also the God who hides himself. He is not some lackey to be summoned when foul weather approaches. Silence is the prerogative of God and by hiding himself from us he weans us from creating him in our own image. Faith means living without answers to some of the core questions in our lives. We concede to God the benefit of mystery if we uphold his sovereignty. Prayers in and of themselves, however, cleanse the heart and provide moments of deep reflection. Sheldon Blank concludes that this "silence is fraught with heavy consequences" and out of it evolves "fortitude and a purification of . . . desires."[54] Richard Foster's words encourage us in the hours and days of spiritual confusion: "Bleak deserts of barrenness and dark canyons" are often experienced by those "who have travelled far into the interior realms of faith."[55]

The cost of ministry

A third principle located in Jeremiah's spiritual crisis is that of having the courage to embrace the daunting cost of prophethood. The messenger of God has an unenviable task although R. E. O. White ventures that "to be allowed to be of use is privilege enough."[56] We serve God on his terms, not ours. We are accountable; he is not. We may have to live with a why. In addition, God demands not merely a witness via *charismata* and word but also through our humanity. Our message must be earthed in flesh and blood and often God preaches his most powerful sermons through the *bios* of the prophet.[57] The world reads with intense interest the parables and object lessons of our life sagas.

The incarnation of the servant's message leads inevitably to alienation, vulnerability, and suffering. For ministry is a call to crisis, conflict, courage, and the cross. The path of prophethood passes via Calvary and the servant becomes a model of the Suffering Servant.[58]

Joseph Mihelic agrees that the confessions permit "not only a glimpse into a prophet's suffering soul in his darkest hour, but through them we are also allowed a glance into the heart of God."[59] Terence Fretheim continues this argument:

> *God is present and active not only in and through what the prophet speaks, but also in what he does and, indeed, in who he is. The prophet's life is an embodiment of the Word of God; the prophet is a*

vehicle for divine immanence. The prophet's life is thus theomorphic.[60]

Ministry is not about theory, speculation, and posturing, but a bitter struggle necessitating combat in the trenches of life and the willingness to come out scarred. We do well to allow God the privilege of dictating the terrain of our ministry because too often the success psychology of our secular society prescribes the expectant character of our service. Our failure in the ministry may be God's vote of success. The called prophet jettisons his rights to dignity and a protective hedge. The first day of our spring disguises the winters of bleak despair and discontent that will follow. God's purposes are inscrutable and the prophet learns that the Lord of heaven and earth holds his cards close to his chest.

Prophets are called to self-abandonment and are not exempt from the hazards of crossing secular humanity. Hours of crisis test the foundation of the servant's faith and the content of his spirituality. When faith is fractured and the prophetic heart is shattered then the kernel of commitment is weighed in the balances. Gerald Janzen demonstrates this point and interprets Jeremiah's confession as enacting a "Joban steadfastness in which doubt and patience define one another and in which even the momentary wish for non-existence is but the dark coloration of the light of faith and unquenchable vocation."[61]

For those of us who profited under the comforts and security of an apartheid system for several years, this principle of cost is confrontational. One must ask pointedly: What risks did we take to identify and support the past disenfranchised and hurting members of our community? Even within the Baptist family, acceptance among the different ethnic groups took time. Our public voice against the evils of apartheid was somewhat muted or hamstrung by bureaucratic machinery. Often our "radical" pronouncements for justice were caught in the slipstream of government initiatives and our Baptist constituency waited in the wings for denominational statesmanship. Will history record our timidity and reticence?

The call to servanthood is not merely a verbalization of the tenets of equity and justice but an actualization of these ideals within our microcosm. A token identification yields a guilty verdict, for Jeremiah's "living sermon" cries out for a faith transplanted in the heart of opposition and the heat of battle. The prophet is in every dimension of his being to serve as exemplar. Jeremiah's stand does not afford the modern-day prophet the luxury of closeting himself behind his church's closed doors. He has to act, react, and interpret public life in the streets and suburbs beyond the shadow of the church's steeple. Jeremiah's life and ministry addressed profoundly public events and he spoke the "truth into a world of falsehood and self-deception."[62] Authentic prophets are compelled to take the harder reading of life's manuscripts, for friendship with God is a costly business.

There will be moments in the routine of ministry when we feel that the stars are out and the pieces dislocated in life's puzzle. We know, as well, how hard it is to preach when our hearts are broken. For Jeremiah's message foretold of a death in history —the nullification of the Exodus, the collapse of Hebrew history and the imminent tragedy of the Exile. Klaus Koch recognizes that "there is a tide in the events of history which even a God may not stay."[63] It is difficult to offer up self-vindication and the right of redress on the altar when people collide with us and unjustly attack our ministry. But we need to take heart: God is in the business of making oak trees, not flimsy reeds.

At times we may feel that the title "Reverend" has banished us to the wastelands of isolation. Mother Teresa stated unequivocally that the worst disease was "not Aids, leprosy or cancer but loneliness."[64] We have to learn to minister in the shadows and in the sunshine, to persevere amidst the weary cycle of ministry. There will be times when we long to abdicate, to run up the white flag and surrender, and to withdraw from the prophetic office and become a "citizen among citizens."[65] The life of the prophet is not for cowards. The faint-hearted will struggle to survive. Key words in the pastor's vocabulary of survival are "endurance" and "resilience." Bernhard Anderson confirms the texture borne out of a life of suffering: "[The confessions] served as a public witness to the prophet's commission as one who, in a special way, was called to walk through 'the valley of deep darkness' (Ps 23:4) with the divine assurance 'I am with you' and in the confidence that vindication lay ahead."[66]

In a sense, Jeremiah touches the chords of God's heart. The Hebrew prophet cannot distance himself from the pain and struggle within God's person. He is not an indifferent spectator to divine pathos. He has caught a glimpse of God's heart in spasm as justice and mercy collide and contest the destiny of Judah. Conflict rages on earth but also reverberates within the Creator's heart in heaven. Through his existential crisis and solitariness, Jeremiah discovered an empathy and an understanding of the ontological suffering and alienation of Yahweh as a deserted covenant partner.[67]

Jeremiah, like Jacob, wrestled with God and stood firm, steadfast, persevering to the end. The prophet may have "spoken in weakness but he acted in strength" and "however much of anguish and despair the 'confessions' may express, these were not the words of a quitter!"[68] When the Jeremianic tradition runs out into the Egyptian desert sand with the abduction of the prophet by Judean fugitives after the fall of Jerusalem in 587 B.C., he is still prophesying (ch.44). Jeremiah journeyed on with God, despite the pain and the incurable wound. His ministry was a foretaste of Golgotha. His confessions stand as testimonials to the authenticity of the prophetic word: an illustration of divine punishment meted out upon a spiritually bankrupt nation rather than as an example of divine powerlessness.[69]

The First Conclusion

Eavesdropping on Jeremiah's dialogue with God gives us confidence to embark upon our own dialogue with God in our own day. Indeed, John Bright draws our attention to the lesson that God "does not extend his call only to the brave, to the saintly, to those who are strangers to doubt and despair. Rather, it pleases him to entrust the treasure of his word to 'earthen vessels.' It is precisely in their weakness and frailty—even in their rebellion—that God calls his servants."[70] For "at least if you are 'battling with God' you still believe that there is someone there with whom it is important and worthwhile to do battle . . . . in truth."[71]

Postscript - Twenty Years Later: A New Introduction

Almost two decades later, the geography has changed from Southern Africa to East Tennessee and the contours of life's journey have taken this writer through some dark shadows and valleys. Within three months of moving to Fort Worth, Texas in 1999 to take up the task of professor and later Dean of Theology at Southwestern Baptist Theological Seminary, we learned that my wife had cancer. Her courage and resolute spirit during the year of radiation and chemotherapy inspired many. I will not forget watching the "toxic" chemical cocktail nicknamed "the red devil" make its way down the plastic bag and attached line into her port during her first chemo treatment. I remember the seventeenth day after her treatment when her hair fell out and she wept with brokenness. But she is a cancer survivor!

A decade later our twenty-three year old daughter Kristen died on August 22 in a tragic event leaving behind Abigail, her beautiful two-year old daughter. That day changed our lives forever. We are survivors but only just . . . and we will limp like Jacob for the rest of our days. Part of me died that day and the lens through which I now view life has moved irrevocably. The following thoughts are part of my grief pilgrimage and protest against that dark day whose shadow lingers on.

Reflecting on the Assault of Death

Naiveté clings to the erroneous presumption that God will spare his own from the assault of personal tragedy. This premise operates even more so when one has given years of service in teaching or ministry on a far off mission field. What spiritual arrogance it is to expect immunity from the dark shadow of death and suffering. Church history is littered with the broken and bloodied corpses of men and women whose only crime was to speak and shine out the light of Christ. But God, I protested this was not my life that ebbed away in the early hours of that dark Saturday morning. It was the life of my youngest child, my daughter. Were you not on watch that night? Did you not hear her desperate cries and understand her brooding, reckless heart? If she had died with cancer or in a car wreck, the brokenness would have been more than we could bear, but compounding the grief is the waste of a young life and the loneliness of the way she died. Who was there to hold her hand and hear her sobs as she lay dying?

Goethe's words haunt me, "What is past cannot return; but if it went down brightly, there is a long afterglow."[72] There is no afterglow with Kris' passing, only the image of her lying cold and still in the funeral parlor. The finality of death is shattering. Why is there an impenetrable wall of separation; an infinite chasm that cannot be crossed? No final parting, no goodbye!

Such visceral questions are laid at the feet of God. But what is it that lies behind them? Do I really want an answer? I am reminded of a chapter in N. T. Wright's book *For All God's Worth* entitled, "The God I Want?"[73] He describes with surgical precision how "the god I want" is a god who is a projection of my own desires, one that will give me what I want, at least at the point of underwriting my existential crises with rational answers.

The problem is that we draw this god with stunted imagination and all idols start out life as the god somebody wanted. If this God is not domesticated he is often caricatured as a distant and remote being that leaves us to muddle through our lives as best we can. Wright states this attitude asserts "the cat's asleep upstairs, and the mice—and perhaps the rats—are organizing the world downstairs."[74] He warns of such a dangerous practice— "Nobody falls down on their face before the god they wanted. Nobody trembles at the word of a home-made god. Nobody goes out with fire in their belly to heal the sick, to clothe the naked, to teach the ignorant, to feed the hungry, because of the god they wanted. They are more likely to stay at home with their feet up."[75]

Phillip Yancey acknowledges that "in grief, love and pain converge."[76] For days and weeks the pain of Kristen's death oscillated between feeling like my chest was ripped open by barbed wire or like that of a man running along a riverbed underwater trying to surface for air. Those physical symptoms yielded to a journey into the desert wasteland of aridity and emotional malaise. The thick fog of lostness engulfed my soul. I wanted to lick my wounds and sit covered in ashes on the mourner's bench. Inertia, dullness, void were the diet of my daily bread.

I remembered in those early dark days the moving words of eighteen-year old Noa Ben Artzi, the granddaughter of Yitzak Rabin, who spoke before the leaders of the world at his funeral in November of 1995. Her moving eulogy touched the watching and listening world. "One always wakes up from a nightmare," she said, "but since yesterday I have only awakened to a nightmare . . . . How do you console a nation when grandma does not stop weeping . . . . Grandfather you were the pillar of fire before the camp, now the camp is in darkness and sadness. The ground has slipped away from under our feet, and we are trying somehow to sit in the empty space that has been left behind."[77]

I did not want to awake for months after Kris' passing. The light of day was a brutal reality that my life was fractured and my daughter gone. I hated every Friday night at midnight into Saturday as I lay awake replaying in my mind what those last hours must have been like for my daughter. I asked myself many questions: "How does one go on? How does one take a step or vote for life?" Nicholas Wolterstorff, who lost his son in a tragic climbing accident in Europe, writes that he has learned to "live around the gap."[78] My courtship with grief has not reached that point. I cannot look at my daughter's photograph for too long because the nerves are too raw and exposed. I must find places to weep in silence and learn self-control when my now four-year old granddaughter takes her mother's picture off my study desk and holds it to her heart and then kisses it.

All of my life, all of my memories are now marked by a single day: pre-and-post August 22, 2009. The lines of George Herbert's poetry in "The Flower" taunt me: "Grief melts away like snow in May, as if there were no such cold thing."[79] My grief is not so easily assuaged. This assault on life consigns me to a path not travelled. It is a new frontier. I wanted no companions as I travelled down this private road. I determined to withdraw into an introspective gulag. My melancholic mood cried out to bring on the darkness and let my "grief smother me like an avalanche."[80] Life's content seemed trivial and petty when measured against this recent grief. I felt adrift, swept out to sea by the currents of grief and barely able to tread water. It took months before I decided to swim towards the shore and then stand on a reef on a "rock that is higher than I."[81] But the sea of loss will always lap around the corridors of my life.

Dealing with Pain

Thomas touched the scars of the resurrected Jesus and caught a glimpse of solidarity in the sacrificial love on the cross. That truth lifted a skeptic out of the abyss of the dark night of doubt and set him on solid ground. I have prayed repeatedly: God, help me to touch your scars. Help me to begin to understand the meaning of this loss of sacred life and how to re-live again. Remind me that "the tears of God are the meaning of history."[82] Remind me that if I could ever see the face of God there would be a tear on your cheek.[83]

Strangely now, death is not a fear but a friend that will introduce me to the One who conquered death and, I trust, the one who left us bereft too soon. The unnatural act of burying your children is like crawling on your knees over broken glass. Yet there is a sense that part of eternity is lodged in my heart. There will be a family reunion and the wings of God's mercy and grace are large enough for her and for me.

In the meantime God will permit honest dissent. He will allow us to rail against the capricious turn of life's road from safety and sunshine into the abyss of darkness and despair. But he will not allow us to travel light. He will recast every sinew and fiber of our spiritual being on the potter's wheel. He will not answer with clear and rational propositions. Why should he? Thomas Merton provides a salutary warning to those of us who expect divine clichés: "If you have found God too easily then perhaps it is not God that you have found."[84] G. B. Caird, Oxford tutor and mentor of Tom Wright, echoes a similar sentiment that "man must know God or perish, but unless he knows God as ultimate mystery, he does not know him at all."[85]

He will, however, give us a flicker of hope: "the blessing of the nadir."[86] Walther Zimmerli defines this idea as "the possibility of new beginnings, beginnings that avoid the mistakes of earlier epochs."[87] I have longed and yearned for just one more conversation with my daughter but that is impossible in this life. I would again tell her how much she was loved. But now there is a new covenant and these words of love are transferred daily to Abby: eye to eye, heart to heart. Remind your own flesh and blood each day that they are loved. Hold those gifts from God close to your heartbeat and cheek. Remember another visit, another lecture, another sermon, and another committee will always throw down the pressure and obligation to compromise your family space. Choose well and hold lightly to your ambitions.

The reality and finality of the crushing invasion and assault of death leaves the survivor reeling with a handful of relevant questions. Much of the substance of past life seems consigned to the realm of the trivial and irrelevant. Looking into the jaws of death has a way of shattering the vase of much of the content of our lives. Now the priorities are settled with clarity. Who do I love? Who makes my world real? Who matters most to me? Perhaps, there is one last sermon to preach. It would be to remember that God is in the process of not only rebuilding out of the rubble of our lives but he is also at prayer remembering our story and our names. The sent one, the divine apostle, the divine revealer, and the redeemer who witnessed Nathaniel "under the fig tree" was also the one who promised the raw and impetuous Galilean fisherman, "Simon, Simon, behold Satan has demanded permission to sift you like wheat, but I have prayed for you that your faith may not fail, and you when once you have turned again, strengthen your brothers."[88]

This Jesus is the One who promises to exchange "ashes for tears."

It is in the travail of the most profound despair—when one is stripped naked and broken—that one can slowly begin to edge towards hope and spiritual awareness. The Danish philosopher, Sören Kierkegaard, declared that "the greater the degree of consciousness, the more intense the despair."[89] In the paradox of loss there is the reminder of the seeking, searching, suffering God who understands and experiences our pain. Truly, grief is hammered out on the anvil of despair and it takes months to move from a profound loss that numbs the spiritual appetite. Gradually with the passing of days one finds a glimpse of resurrection hope. I visit Kris' grave often and in those moments have thought of the one who touched the coldness and stillness of death with lingering hope. For the Son of Man confronted death long before the agony of Gethsemane and Golgotha.

In his day, Jesus travelled into the world of professional mourners and confronted Jairus' crisis of grief. He found privacy in that moment and touched the official's little girl with words of life. He spoke tenderly in Aramaic *talitha cum* paraphrased "little lamb get up." Isaiah writes in the midst of his soliloquy on God's creative fiat, majesty, and power of Yahweh's mercy in 40:11. The prophet speaks of God carrying in his bosom the exiles as lambs. The word for "lamb" in the Hebrew text may also be used of a little child and this is the word Jesus uses of the daughter of Jairus, "talitha."[90] The word "bosom" refers to the "fold of the shepherd's robe which can be a natural pocket to shelter a lamb."[91] The compassion of the Father and Son come through in the Isaianic and Marcan passage. When I stand at the grave of my daughter I pray "Lord, please look after our little lamb."

Travelling five miles south-east of Nazareth, Jesus and his disciples encountered a funeral cortege. A widow had been struck a double blow—death of a husband and now the son. In a village of this size death touches everyone. The lifeless body would be carried a short distance to a cave and placed inside on the main ledge next to an ossuary containing the folded bones of the father. It is to this place of death the funeral procession marches. Amidst this vulnerability and grief Jesus comes and touches the bier. Clean and unclean classifications are meaningless to him. His touch gives life. When I stand at the grave of my daughter, I am reminded of Helmut Thielicke's words in his Easter sermon entitled "Time and Eternity:"

> "*Oceans of this uncertain world are no more than a puddle in the hand of my Savior, The continents and mountains are only an ear of corn in His finger. And this hand is the hand of the victor. One day when all human hands have fallen and perished it will be stretched over the earth as the first hand. In a royal gesture it will open the graves and summon the skeletons to Him.*"[92]

Bethany marks another place of life in the midst of the pall of death. The friend of Jesus lies entombed for several days before Jesus arrives. Mary and Martha and the crowd believe they stand in the presence of death but in fact they stand in the presence of life. If the raw power of the Sea of Galilee is muzzled with an injunction, then at his command the stupor of death is interrupted and Lazarus walks out of his tomb alive. When I stand at the grave of my daughter I recall the tears of the rabbi from the backwater of Nazareth as he encountered Mary and all the Judeans with her. Here was the Son of Man in solidarity with the fragility of the broken heart. As he stood in that little village at Lazarus' tomb he stands with me up a hill at my daughter's grave nestled in the Greenwood cemetery beside three crosses.

The German theologian Helmut Thielicke declared "a breach has been made in the impregnable wall of death" and he inquired "where else can we go but to the open grave in the vicinity of Calvary."[93] Before we can get there, however, we walk away from the sight of a closed grave that has violently snatched part of our own dreams and flesh and blood away. The neat tapestry of our lives is rent asunder together with the dissonance marking this event that cries out with the reality of abandonment. It was there two thousand years ago on skull hill. The silence and non-intervention of God is the real abandonment that Jesus endures on the cross. Let us never forget at what cost the crucified God has become the brother of the despised, abandoned, oppressed, and grief-stricken. Martelet writes that the "why" unleashed from the crucified Jesus on the cross intercepts and holds in trust my "why." Movingly, he asserted:

> *Christ has sunk the shaft of his cross so deep into the sea, with it he has explored the unfathomable depths of the human ocean to such an extent that there exists no pain, no darkness, no loneliness, no contempt of others or of oneself, no horror, no abandonment, no cry, nothing except hell itself which is the absurd negation of this salvific love, nothing at all that is not found in him who has not refused anything of the misery he finds in us.*[94]

The words of William Blake in "The Auguries of Innocence" encapsulate the struggle of humankind as we experience the bright and dark side of life. The English poet, painter, engraver, and visionary wrote that "joy and woe were woven fine."[95] Signing up for life means that we cannot travel on a road of sunshine indefinitely. Sooner or later we will reach a moment of "ground zero" like Jeremiah. We will stop and stagger under the load of grief. This assault will demand that we lay down the tools of life and stumble around in the shadows awhile and during that sabbatical of crisis discover God in our broken places.

David Atkinson writes of a young Jewish lad who wrote on the walls of the Warsaw ghetto during the Second World War: "I believe in the sun, even if it does not shine, I believe in love, even if I do not feel it, I believe in God, even if I do not see him."[96] Almost two thousand years earlier a Jewish man from the village of Nazareth who preached the radical news of the breaking in of God's kingdom hung outside Jerusalem's city gates on a brutal cross. His message was clear in this act that splices history into two spheres and two ways. His act of incarnate love and suffering grief, then as now, reaches down to hold me steady as I carve out tracks from my barren wilderness of loss toward an oasis of living water.

Notes

[1]The first section of this chapter, with some amendments here, was published in *The South African Baptist Journal of Theology* (1994), 74-93 and is used with permission from the editor.

[2]Louis McBurney, *Every Pastor Needs a Pastor* (Marble, Colorado: Louis McBurney, 1977), 97.

[3]H. B. London accuses suffocating expectations of locking "pastor and congregations into dismal relational prisons" (*Pastors at Risk* [Wheaton: Victor Books, 1993], 41).

[4]E. W. Heaton, *The Old Testament Prophets* (London: Darton, Longman, and Todd, 1977), 44. Joseph L. Mihelic posits that "originally these confessions may have been a part of a personal diary which he may have kept during the years of seclusion (608-598 B.C.) when he was hiding from Jehoiakim's police" ("Dialogue with God," *Interpretation* 14 [1960], 43).

[5]Walter Brueggemann warns: "The critical problems concerning the relation of the *person* of Jeremiah to the *Book* of Jeremiah are notoriously difficult. There seems to be no great progress on that question in current scholarship ("The Book of Jeremiah: Portrait of the Prophet," *Interpretation* 37 [1983], 130). In

corroboration, L. G. Perdue admits that "the 'Confessions' have been the source of the greatest controversy in regard to the quest for the historical Jeremiah" ("Jeremiah in Modern Research: Approaches and Issues," *A Prophet to the Nations: Essays in Jeremiah Studies*, eds. L. G. Perdue and B. W. Kovacs [Winona Lake, Indiana: Eisenbrauns, 1984], 25). The major interpretive approaches in confession-research include the following:

(1) the **psychological-biographical model** that understands these dialogues as a recording of the prophet's private prayers and inner spiritual struggles occasioned by the hardship and tensions of his prophetic role (Walter Baumgartner, John Skinner, John Berridge, Sheldon Blank, John Bright, William Holladay, and Joseph Mihelic);

(2) the **cultic-mediator paradigm** rejects the confessions as psychological transcripts and Jeremiah becomes the cultic spokesman for a community lament directed towards God. The individual "I" is swallowed up in the collective "We" and the figure of the prophetic individual fades into that of the anonymous liturgist (H. Graf Reventlow);

(3) the **redactional-interpretation method** considers the confessions and the person of Jeremiah given to us as a reconstruction by Deuteronomic editors. The tradents have shaped a Jeremianic figure contextualized within and for the needs of the exilic community (Ernest W. Nicholson, Robert Carroll, and A. H. J. Gunneweg);

(4) the **synchronic approach** eschews the historicist quest, bypasses the editorial interpretations, and focuses solely on the final form of the text (A. R. Diamond and Timothy Polk).

For a more detailed analysis of the historical and current approaches to the issue of Jeremiah's confessions see A. R. Diamond, "The Confessions of Jeremiah in Context: Scenes of Prophetic Drama," *Journal for the Study of the Old Testament Supplement Series* 45 (1987), 11-16 and Leo G. Perdue, "Jeremiah in Modern Research," 24-27. For the purposes of this article we will follow the first model of interpretation drawing on Bright's statement that "it has remained well-nigh the consensus among scholars that the Confessions do in some way relate to specific experiences in the life of the prophet" ("Jeremiah's Complaints: Liturgy, or Expressions of Personal Distress?" in *Proclamation and Presence: Old Testament Essays in Honor of Gwynne Henton Davies*, eds. John I. Durham and J. R. Porter [Macon, Georgia: Mercer University Press, 1970], 190). Samuel Balentine supports the psychological-biographical model, claiming that "attributing his prayers to a later editor or by subordinating the role of Jeremiah the individual supplicant to that of Jeremiah the cultic prophet who prays not for himself but for the community at large . . . dissolves the prophet Jeremiah into anonymity" ('Jeremiah, Prophet of Prayer," *Review and Expositor* 78 [Summer 1981], 334). Walter Brueggemann concedes that "it is also probable that the person, memory, and impact of Jeremiah were so powerful and enduring that that personal reality presided over and shaped the imaginative reconstruction . . . . That reconstruction is not historically precise, but it is not literarily fanciful, undisciplined, or cut loose from its referent" ("The Book of Jeremiah,"131-132).

[6]Geoffrey Hartman, "Jeremiah 20:7-12: A Literary Response," *The Biblical Mosaic: Changing Perspectives*, eds. Robert Polzin and Eugene Rothman (Philadelphia: Fortress Press, 1982), 194.

[7]Joel Gregory commends his fidelity to the task at hand: "No man in history could have possibly served God with greater integrity in more difficult circumstances with more complete surrender and undivided loyalty than the prophet Jeremiah" (*Growing Pains of the Soul* [New York: Guideposts, 1978], 18-19).

[8]Kathleen O'Connor argues: "These splendid poems capture . . . human experience which has a universal quality" and "the suffering of Jeremiah serves as a paradigm of the innocent suffering of believers. The confessions have been so prominent in Christian life and piety precisely because this is so" (*The*

Confessions of Jeremiah: Their Interpretation and Their Role in Chapters 1-25 [Atlanta: Scholars Press, 1988], 235).

[9]We shall follow the biblical ordering of the five confessions: 11:18-12:6; 15:10-21; 17:12-18; 18:18-23; and 20:7-18. As to terminology, the traditional title of "confessions" will be maintained. Other descriptions include:

(1) "laments" drawing attention to the influence of the genre of individual lament located in the Psalms and the prophet's deeply felt sense of alienation (W. Baumgartner),

(2) "complaints" highlighting the element of conflict in the prophetic vocation and woundedness in relationship with God (W. Holladay),

(3) "prayers" defining the form and content of these dialogues with an address to God, a lament and petition for deliverance or relief (S. Blank).

Peter Craigie rightly points out that "neutral terminology does not exist" and each term "presupposes a different understanding about their nature and purpose" (*Jeremiah 1-25* in *Word Biblical Commentary* [Dallas: Word, 1991], 26A:173).

[10]Gerhard von Rad, "The Confessions of Jeremiah," *Theodicy in the Old Testament* ed. James L. Crenshaw (Philadelphia: Fortress Press, 1983), 95.

[11]James Ward contends that "a plausible setting for the complaint contained in 20:7-18 has been provided by the editorial placement of this passage immediately after 20:1-6" (*The Prophets*, eds. Lloyd Bailey and Victor Furnish [Nashville: Abingdon Press, 1982], 68). Ronald Clements concurs: "The occasion of Jeremiah's public beating and humiliation in the stocks provides the background for the last of the prophet's so-called confessions (20:7-13)" (*Jeremiah* in *Interpretation* [Atlanta: John Knox Press, 1988], 120).

[12]Sheldon H. Blank, "The Confessions of Jeremiah and the Meaning of Prayer," *Hebrew Union College Annual* 21 (1948), 348.

[13] Mihelic, "Dialogue with God," 47.

[14]John Bright, *Jeremiah* in *The Anchor Bible* (New York: Doubleday, 1965), 132; contra D. J. A. Clines and D. M. Gunn, "'You Tried to Persuade Me' and 'Violence! Outrage!' in Jeremiah 20:7-8," *Vetus Testamentum* 28 (1978), 20-27.

[15]W. Baumgartner, *Die Klagegedichte des Jeremia* (Giessen: Alfred Topelmann, 1917), 64.

[16]Abraham Heschel defines the struggle: "The prophet feels both the attraction and coercion of God, the appeal and the pressure, the charm and the stress. He is conscious of both voluntary identification and forced capitulation" (*The Prophets*, 2 vols. [New York: Harper and Row, 1962], 1:114); Von Rad likewise interprets Jeremiah's calling as not a question of inner conviction of right or wrong but "a question of power pure and simple" namely, "a fearfully unequal power relationship" ("The Confessions of Jeremiah," 94).

[17]Robert Davidson, *The Courage to Doubt* (London: SCM, 1983), 137.

[18]John Bright, "A Prophet's Lament and Its Answer: Jeremiah15:10-21," *Interpretation* 28 (1974), 66.

[19]Von Rad captures the spirit of the prophet's dilemma: "God enticed Jeremiah the way a watercourse enticingly beckons flocks and tents. For a time it went well—but then it was like being taken in; a trust had been betrayed" ("The Confessions of Jeremiah," 90).

[20]Richard Jacobson, "Prophecy and Paradox," *Linguistica Biblica* 38 (1976), 58.

[21]Michael Fishbane, "A Wretched Thing of Shame, A Mere Belly: An Interpretation of Jeremiah 20:7-12," *The Biblical Mosaic: Changing Perspectives*, eds. Robert Polzin and Eugene Rothman (Philadelphia: Fortress Press, 1982), 173-174.

[22]Jacobson, "Prophecy and Paradox," 51-52.

[23]Klaus Koch remarks: "The man from Anathoth knows that he has been forced into a role which in no way corresponds to his own personal leanings. Shy and sensitive as he is, the intrigues carried on behind his back chafe him more than the physical deprivations and external sufferings which were to be their result" (*The Prophets*, 2 vols. [London: SCM, 1983], 2:43).

[24]Fishbane, "A Wretched Thing of Shame," 173.

[25]Willem Vangemeren states that Jeremiah "struggled with his God, with his mission, and with God's message" (*Interpreting the Prophetic Word* [Grand Rapids: Academie, 1990], 299).

[26]Brueggemann, "The Book of Jeremiah," 142.

[27]Bernhard Anderson suggests another reason why Jeremiah's home town was hostile toward him: "The passage . . . may reflect the fierce animosity of the people of Anathoth, who were aroused perhaps, by his advocacy of a reform program that threatened to put local priests out of their jobs" (*The Living World of the Old Testament* [Harlow: Longman, 1988], 407). Richard Jacobson comments "earlier prophets such as Elijah had won the enmity of kings, only Jeremiah suffers the stab in the back at home" ("Prophecy and Paradox," 57).

[28]Clyde Francisco interprets the prophet's social status of bachelorhood and withdrawal from community and social events, such as weddings and funerals, as signifying that an "odor of death" hangs over the nation of Judah (*Studies in Jeremiah* [Nashville: Convention Press, 1961], 67).

[29]Fishbane, "A Wretched Thing of Shame," 177.

[30]Walther Zimmerli, *Old Testament Theology in Outline* (Edinburgh: T. and T. Clark, 1978), 206. W. L. Holladay contends that Jeremiah's confessions represent in essence the prophet's suit against God for breach of contract: "The problem of theodicy for Jeremiah, then, is not why do the innocent suffer
. . . [but] *why do thy mockers* (and thus my mockers) *continue to thrive*" ("Jeremiah's Lawsuit with God," *Interpretation* 17 [1963], 286).

[31]Davidson, *The Courage to Doubt*, 124.

[32]Heschel, *The Prophets*, 121.

[33]Brueggemann, "The Book of Jeremiah," 133, 142.

[34]Some scholars see 20:14-18 as an independent unit or invert the order by placing 14-18 before 7-13 (Ewald, Cornill, Schmidt et al). Donald Wimmer argues that sudden emotional and intellectual shifts are natural in such struggles and he upholds the unity of the confession ("The Sociology of Knowledge and 'The Confessions of Jeremiah,'" *SBL Seminar Papers* [1978] 1: 405).

[35]E. W. Heaton declares that "this terrible cry of dereliction—like that other cry from a cross of suffering six hundred years later—is not a denial of the prophet's vocation, but the very strongest confirmation of its depth" (*The Old Testament Prophets*, 45). Similarly, Sheldon Blank writes: "His 'why?' is not addressed to God. It is less a question than a whimper . . . . It is not really the fact of his existence that has upset him, it is the use to which his life has been put. It is from what he and God have made of his life that he wants to run away" ("The Confessions of Jeremiah and the Meaning of Prayer," 352-353).

[36]Anderson, *The Living World of the Old Testament*, 409.

[37]Davidson, *The Courage to Doubt*, 139.

[38]Balentine, "Jeremiah, Prophet of Prayer," 334.

[39]J. P. Hyatt, *Interpreters Bible* (1956), 5:783.

[40]R. E. O. White, *The Indomitable Prophet: A Biographical Commentary on Jeremiah* (Grand Rapids: William B. Eerdmans Publishing Company, 1992), 161.

[41]Vangemeren, *Interpreting the Prophetic Word,* 301.

[42]Ward, *The Prophets*, 72.

[43]Bright, "A Prophet's Lament and Its Answer," 69. Samuel Balentine comments on the significance that Jeremiah's accusing questions are framed within the context of prayer and the prophet "approached God with what he really felt, not with what he thought God wanted to hear" ("Jeremiah, Prophet of Prayer," 340). John Skinner concurs: "But to Jeremiah prayer is more than petition. It is intimate conversation with God, in which his whole inner life is laid bare, with its perplexities and struggles and temptations, and he unburdens himself of the distress which weighs down his spirit, in the sure confidence that he is heard and understood by the God to whom all things are naked and open" (*Prophecy and Religion* [Cambridge: Cambridge University Press, 1922], 213-214).

[44]Eugene H. Peterson, *Run with Horses* (Downers Grove: IVP, 1983), 103.

[45]Gregory, *Growing Pains of the Soul*, 25.

[46]Balentine, "Jeremiah, Prophet of Prayer," 331.

[47]Timothy Polk, “The Prophetic Persona: Jeremiah and the Language of the Self,” *Journal for the Study of the Old Testament Supplement Series* 32 (1984), 208.

[48]Gerhard von Rad, *Old Testament Theology*, trans. D. M. G. Stalker. 2 vols. (London: SCM, 1965), 2:206.

[49]The late Steve Biko, who died in detention on 12 September 1977, sought a new black consciousness and renaissance in South Africa. His voice declared with insight: “Enabling people to 'walk tall' and with dignity calls for a psychological revolution in the black community. Three hundred years of racial and economic oppression have generated deeply ingrained stereotypes of a negative kind. No man can wage a meaningful war of liberation unless and until he has effectively eradicated his 'slave mentality' and his feelings of inadequacy” (*Contending Ideologies in South Africa*, eds. James Leatt, Theo Kneifel, and Klaus Nürnberger [Cape Town: David Philip, 1986], 108). Charles Villa-Vicencio cites Biko' s provocative words: “All in all the black man [sic] has become a shell, a shadow of a man, completely defeated, drowning in his own misery, a slave, an ox bearing the yoke of oppression with sheepish timidity. . . . The first step therefore is to make the black man come to himself; to pump back life into his empty shell; to infuse him with pride and dignity, to remind him of his complicity in the crime of allowing himself to be misused and therefore letting evil reign in the country of his birth” (*Civil Disobedience and Beyond* [Cape Town: David Philip, 1990], 122).

[50]O'Connor, “The Confessions of Jeremiah,” 233.

[51]*Ibid.*, 236.

[52]Peterson, *Run with the Horses*, 103-104.

[53]Balentine, “Jeremiah, Prophet of Prayer,” f. n. 26.

[54]Blank, "The Confessions of Jeremiah and the Meaning of Prayer," 354.
[55]Richard Foster writes: "I want you to know that to be faced with the 'withering winds of God's hiddenness' does not mean that God is displeased with you, or that you are insensitive to the work of God's Spirit, or that you have committed some horrendous offence against heaven, or that there is something wrong with you, or anything. Darkness is a definite experience of prayer. It is to be expected, even embraced" (*Prayer: Finding the Heart's True Home* [Cape Town: Struik, 1992], 19).

[56]White, *The Indomitable Prophet*, 158.

[57]Von Rad states that Jeremiah's "suffering soul, his life bleeding to death in God's task—all this becomes a pointer towards God" ("The Confessions of Jeremiah," 98). In fact, Sheldon Blank posits that these protests of Jeremiah's private life become public property because this prophet serves as an analogy and paradigm for subsequent generations ("The Prophet as Paradigm," in *Prophetic Essays and Addresses* [Cincinnati: Hebrew Union College Press, 1977], 23-34). Compare John Thompson who states: "It was not easy to determine when the dialogs and monologs were produced. It is most unlikely that they were declared publicly. They may have been revealed to Baruch or to some intimate friends or even committed to writing" (*The Book of Jeremiah in The New International Commentary on the Old Testament* [Grand Rapids: William B. Eerdmans Publishing Company, 1980], 91). He holds to the position that most of the confessions reflect the severe tensions of the prophet's life in the days of Jehoiakim.

[58]John Berridge argues that "Yahweh's coming judgment was not only verbally proclaimed by Jeremiah, but it was also necessary that this judgment be symbolically portrayed in his own life" (*Prophet, People and the Word of Yahweh* in *Basel Studies of Theology* [Zürich: EVZ, 1970], 155).

[59]Mihelic, "Dialogue with God," 50.

[60]Terence Fretheim states: "The people thus not only hear the Word of God from the prophet, they see the Word enfleshed in their midst. In and through the suffering of the prophet, the people both hear and see God immersed in human experience. Through the prophet, Israel relates not only to a God who speaks but also to a God who appears" (*The Suffering of God* [Philadelphia: Fortress Press, 1984], 165).

[61]J. Gerald Janzen, "Jeremiah 20:7-18," *Interpretation* 37 (1983), 180.

[62]Brueggemann, "The Book of Jeremiah," 144.

[63]Koch, *The Prophets*, 2:45.

[64]London, *Pastors at Risk*, 50.

[65]Von Rad, "The Confessions of Jeremiah," 90.

[66]Anderson, *The Living World of the Old Testament*, 410.

[67]Janzen, "Jeremiah 20:7-18," 181.

[68]Bright, "A Prophet's Lament and Its Answer," 71.

[69]O'Connor sums up the purpose of the confessions: "The purpose of each of the confessions is to authenticate Jeremiah's vocation as a true prophet against the accusations that he was a false prophet" (*The Confessions of Jeremiah*, 232, 238).

[70]Bright, "A Prophet's Lament and Its Answer," 69.

[71]Davidson, *The Courage to Doubt*, 139.

[72]Helmut Thielicke, *The Silence of God* in *A Thielicke Trilogy*, trans. G. W. Bromiley (Grand Rapids, Michigan: William B. Eerdmans Publishing Company, 1962), 192.

[73]N. T. Wright, *For All God's Worth: True Worship and the Calling of the Church* (Grand Rapids, Michigan: William B. Eerdmans Publishing Company, 1997), 23-32.

[74]*Ibid.*, 26.

[75]*Ibid.*, 23-24.

[76]Philip Yancey, *What Good is God? In Search of a Faith that Matters* (New York: Faith Words, 2010), 26.

[77]The Jerusalem Report Staff, *Yitzhak Rabin: Soldier of Peace*, ed. David Horowitz (London: Peter Halban, 1996), 213-214. See also Noa Ben-Artzi, "Remembering Rabin: 10 Years Later," [cited 20 October]. http://info.jpost.com/C005/Supplements/Rabin/411.07.html.

[78]Nicholas Wolterstorff, *Lament for a Son* (Grand Rapids, Michigan: William B. Eerdmans Publishing Company, 1987), 99.

[79]George Herbert, *George Herbert: The Complete English Poems* in *Penguin Classics*, ed. John Tobin (London: Penguin Books: 2004), 156.
[80]Yancey, *What Good is God*, 26.

[81]Psalm 61:2.

[82]Wolterstorff, *Lament for a Son*, 90.

[83]Abraham Heschel, *The Ineffable Name of God: Man*, (New York: Continuum International Publishing Company, 2005), 43.

[84]Thomas Merton, *No Man is an Island* (Boston: Shambhala Publications, 2005), 205.

[85]G. B. Caird, *Paul's Letters from Prison: Ephesians* in the *New Clarendon Bible* (Oxford: Oxford University Press, 1981), 70.

[86]Walther Zimmerli, *I Am Yahweh.* ed. Walter Brueggemann, trans. Douglas W. Stott (Atlanta: John Knox Press, 1982), 111.

[87]*Ibid.*

[88] Luke 23:32.

[89]Sören Kierkegaard, *Fear and Trembling and The Sickness Unto Death*, trans. Walter Lowrie (Princeton, New Jersey: Princeton University Press, 1968), 182.

[90]George A. E. Knight, *Servant Theology: Isaiah 40-55* in the *International Theological Commentary* (Grand Rapids, Michigan: William B. Eerdmans Publishing Company 1984), 18.

[91]John D. Watts, *Isaiah 34-66* in the *Word Biblical Commentary*, vol.25 (Waco, Texas: Words Book Publisher, 1987), 90.

[92]Thielicke, *The Silence of God*, 193.

[93]*Ibid.*, 184-185.

[94]G. Martelet, *L'Au-delà retrouvé. Christologie des fins dernières* (Paris: Desclée, 1975) cited by Gerard Rossé, *The Cry of Jesus on the Cross*, trans. Stephen Wentworth Arndt (New York: Paulist Press, 1987), 115-116.

[95]William Blake, *The Complete Poetry and Prose of William Blake*, ed. David

Eerdman and commentary Harold Bloom (New York: Anchor Books, 1998), 491.

[96]David Atkinson, "A Cry of Faith" *Expository Times* 96 (1985), 147.

Living with Pain:
Reflections on Surviving the Loss of a Child

H. Wayne Ballard, Jr., Ph. D.
Associate Professor, School of Religion
Carson-Newman College

Today We Buried a Child[1]

Today my community buried a child. A sad and lamentable thing it was. After only seventeen months of life, Jake is dead. There is no readily apparent cause. The community is saddened and broken.

But it is not disheartened, for it is a Christian community and it is rooted in Biblical faith. Jake was not old enough to have made any of his own decisions about his life; he was being raised in the ways of his mother and father. They are both devoted Christians. They would have done anything, borne any burden, met any expense to save their son, but they did not have the chance. It happened too fast. And Jake's spirit has gone to meet his heavenly Father, while his earthly father and mother lovingly put his physical remains in the earth and turn to meet the demands of raising Jake's two older brothers. The real ministry of the community is about to begin, for in the tough days ahead, this family will need prayers, encouraging words, and thoughtful deeds.

At the funeral, we saw three generations of men in the family, and heard of a fourth—Jake was named for his great-grandfathers. It was so obvious that Jake's grandfather loved him as he spoke about his precious little boy who brought him so much joy. Our grandchildren bring us a unique kind of joy unlike any other experience. Mysteriously, we know that they, as well as their mothers and fathers, are bone of our bone and flesh of our flesh. We seem compelled to hug them and hold them, as if touch is the only way to get close to their vital inner reality.

Jake's father sang in the service. He shared with the rest of the community the privacy of Jake's favorite lullabies, one in Hebrew and one in English. The one in Hebrew came from the Torah; Deuteronomy 6:4 tells Israel to hear that its Lord God is one. Though Jake could not understand Hebrew, his Christian father imparted to him a central truth of the faith in its original language. For Hebrew and Christian alike, the Lord, the Lord our God is one. Jake's father wrote the second one in English, a song to quiet a child on the sometimes uneasy road to sleep, a tune to bring peace through the night. Jake's father sang truth and imparted peace. What a legacy to give a son. Would that all the fathers in our community could learn to give so much of themselves and their love.

The family and the community were ministered to by comforting words, some spoken through tears and deep emotion; by beautiful and poignant music; some from a single stringed instrument; and by prayers. All of these expressions were rooted in the book of our heritage—the Holy Bible. Some of us know it well and some just barely—all are comforted by it. And when we do not understand something in our midst and it looms as inexplicable tragedy, we need to be reassured by ancient words that bring and renew life and hope.

My community will never forget Jake. And we will hold his parents in our hearts in the days to come. Our prayer will be that the Father will draw them very near as well, to impart healing in their suffering, to give blessing in their perseverance, to forge strength for their character, and to ensure renewal in their hope.

Living With the Pain:[2]
Reflections on Surviving the Loss of a Loved One[3]

C. S. Lewis is one of the most profound Christian writers of the twentieth century. He wrote about many things from his famous children stories like the *Chronicles of Narnia* to his devotional musings in his *Reflections on the Psalms.* Lewis completed two works addressing the issue of death and human frailty. In 1940, he completed a highly theoretical work titled *The Problem of Pain.* In the first major chapter of this work Lewis asserts:

> *If God were good, He would wish to make His creatures perfectly happy, and if God were almighty, He would be able to do what He wished. But the creatures are not happy. Therefore God lacks either*

> *goodness, or power, or both. This is the problem of pain, in its simplest form.*[4]

Lewis' answer to the problem of pain was deemed a literary success as it sold over 120,000 copies. The critics claimed the work was "a little too pat."[5] Indeed, as one reads through this work it seems a bit "antiseptic" and trite.

On July 13, 1960, Lewis' wife Joy Davidman Gresham, whom he had married late in life as a confirmed bachelor, died after suffering from cancer. His collection of scattered thoughts and writings about this event were first published under the name N. W. Clerk (a pun from the Old English, meaning "I know not what scholar") with the title, *A Grief Observed*.[6]

Notice now the difference in the words from *The Problem of Pain* as you read from the first two paragraphs of Lewis' own confessional experience with death in *A Grief Observed*, first published in 1961:

> *No one ever told me that grief felt so much like fear. I am not afraid, but the sensation is like being afraid. The same fluttering in the stomach, the same restlessness, the yawning, I keep on swallowing.*
>
> *At other times it feels like being mildly drunk, or concussed. There is a sort of invisible blanket between the world and me. I find it hard to take in what anyone says. Or perhaps, hard to want to take it in. It*

is so uninteresting. Yet I want the others to be about me. I dread the moments when the house is empty. If only they would talk to one another and not to me.[7]

Lewis powerfully reminds us that it is one thing to write theoretically about suffering and pain, and quite another personally to experience loss firsthand. Death becomes more relevant when it happens to someone we care for so deeply. This has certainly been the case for me. I had preached dozens of funerals for others including family members and grandparents. I had visited with families and friends who had just lost loved ones. But I had never discovered the depths of the pain involved when someone so close to you, someone that has been entrusted to your care, has passed away.

The Event

May 7, 2000 was the darkest day of my life. I was sitting in a deacon's meeting at the Westfield Baptist Church of Dunn, North Carolina when our Youth Minister's girlfriend came into the meeting and delivered the news to me that they had taken my youngest son from the nursery of First Baptist Church, Buies Creek, where my wife was the Minister of Children, to Good Hope Hospital in Erwin, North Carolina because Jake had stopped breathing.

I calmly walked out of that meeting and drove across town to the hospital. When I saw the size of the gathering crowd of our friends and colleagues from work, I began to understand the severity of the situation. The Emergency Response workers had responded quickly to the call at the church, but they had been unable to revive Jake, my beloved son of seventeen months. He was "Daddy's Boy." He had just begun to say "Hot" and "Uh Oh." He was walking and talking and developing a great personality. He was the perfect child except for that one day when he decided that instead of blowing on his daddy's belly he would bite into his daddy's belly. That was a bite I will never forget.

Friends drove us home that night from the hospital. There we had to face our older two boys with the grim news that their angelic little brother was gone. Brack, our eldest, was ten. Zachary, our middle son, was six. We simply sat on the family couch and cried. And cried. And cried.

Friends and family came from over a thousand miles away. Church members from our previous ministry positions across the country came and grieved with our family. It was a tremendous outpouring of support and love.

The service was difficult. I wanted to sing Jake to sleep one more time. Jake loved to sit and hear me play my guitar. He was so cute. When we would put on a CD of a great guitarist Jake would point to the speaker and say "Da, Da?" I played a song I wrote simply called a "Lullaby." I also sang the "Night, Night" song, which is the Jewish *Shema* from Deuteronomy 6:4:

Shema, Yisrael, Adonai, Eloheynu, Adonai, Echad.
Hear O Israel, the Lord our God, the Lord is One.

Kim and I chose to use Lamentations 3:19-30 as a central focus of the service. We wanted to affirm the faithfulness of God even though we both questioned whether God had really been faithful to our family. I remember dimly thinking at the graveside committal that this burial could not be happening—that we just needed to open up the casket and that Jake would be all right. But he was not alive! My family was **not** ok! And I was NOT all right!

The Aftershock

I was devastated. There was and is a giant hole left in the middle of my heart. The little boy who brought so much joy and happiness to our family was gone. I often went to his graveside and wanted to tear open the grave and just hold him once again. In many ways it was a multifaceted loss. How was I to deal with this tragedy and really minister and care for my remaining two sons? I was dealing with such powerful emotions and they were dealing with emotions they had never experienced before. The concept of death was a new notion to them. How could I help them when I seemed powerless to help myself? My wife, who has a tremendous voice and was a Vocal Performance music major in college, was unable to sing publicly for the next two years. Even when she tried about the only thing that came out were tears. Our youngest son Zachary could not sleep without every light in the house being illuminated. Even now, twelve years later, we have to follow behind him at night to make sure the lights in every room in the house are not left on when he goes to bed.

The summer of 2000 found the Ballard family spending a lot of time at Wrightsville Beach just outside of Wilmington, North Carolina. A church member where I was interim pastor had a beach front home where we spent most of that summer. Most days were filled with long slow walks on the beach just watching the waves come in and go back out. Other days were spent with me just sitting and staring out at the waves. The waves were incredibly therapeutic.

Our home church, First Baptist Church of Buies Creek and the Westfield Baptist Church of Dunn, North Carolina, were graciously supportive. These two churches held my family up when it seemed that nothing else could.

As time passed I went back to teaching and helping out churches on the weekend as an interim pastor. I also began to read a few books dealing with the loss of a child—Richard Hipps' book *When a Child Dies*[8] was among those books that were recommended to me. This book was given to me two weeks after the funeral by one of my seminary students at the Campbell University Divinity School. Hipps' book was a genuine help at this stage of grief. It reminded me that I was not the first, nor would I be the last, to suffer such a great loss. Nicholas Wolterstorff also has a wonderful book titled *Lament for a Son*[9] that I found to be very honest and helpful during this hour. Another book that I highly recommend to others who are dealing with the loss of a loved one is John Claypool's *Tracks of a Fellow Struggler.*[10] All of these resources help us begin to realize just what we are up against when we lose a loved one.

Finding Solace in Scripture

In 2 Corinthians 4:5-12 the apostle Paul exhorts the Church at Corinth to allow the light of Jesus Christ to shine through their individual hardships and persecutions. A focal verse in this text is verse ten:

> *We always carry around in our body the death of Jesus, so that the life of Jesus may also be revealed in our body*. (2 Cor 4:10; *NIV*)

In light of my personal loss, please allow me the opportunity to interpret 2 Corinthians 4:10 through the lens of my experience. First, when we lose someone we deeply love a real part of us dies. There is a part of me that will never live again. For those who were followers of Jesus Christ a part of them died when Jesus died on the cross—the one that they had followed for the better part of three years was gone. The followers and family of Jesus Christ, like C. S. Lewis and I, experienced the pain only known when you lose someone for whom you deeply care.

Second, it is only when we die to ourselves that Jesus Christ can live through us today. Not a single day goes by that I do not remember Jake, and he lives with me, through me, and in my daily life. As believers, Jesus Christ lives through us today.

In verses eight and nine, Paul expresses the personal anguish and pain that accompanies the struggler in life.

> *We are pressed on every side by troubles, be we are not crushed and broken. We are perplexed, but we don't give up and quit. We are hunted down, but God never abandons us. We get knocked down, but we get up again and keep going.* (2 Cor 4:8-9; *NLT*)

Within the same year of Jake's death, many of our friends were also experiencing their own losses and troubles. Before Jake's death, I sat with Don Garner in the lobby of the Duke University Hospital as his twenty-year old son lay dying from brain injuries suffered in an automobile accident. In the years following Aaron's death, Don expressed that he felt like he always had a subterranean plow dragging behind him deep within the ground. In my loss, it seemed that after the first year I was just beginning to emerge from a deep, dark fog.

One of my wife's best friends, Jill Upshaw, was critically injured in an automobile accident while she was just a few weeks pregnant. She lay in a coma for the next several years before she eventually died. The baby was born and she is a beautiful young lady today. Another of Kim's best friends, Peggy Barker, a mother of two preteens at the time, was diagnosed with liver cancer and she passed away a short time later. Kim and I both experienced personal setbacks in our professional lives. These personal setbacks added to the intensity of our grief rather than providing a healthy outlet for our grief to be expressed.

At some point you begin to look behind you to see if Eliphaz, Bildad, and Zophar are coming over to share their so-called collective wisdom.

We still miss Baby Jake. The moments when I am alone are perhaps the most difficult. But I am thankful for every day of those seventeen months and I would not trade a minute of Jake's life and the moments we shared of his life for anything. Jake would be fourteen this year. In the midst of pain, life does go on.

When the world collapses around you, those words of Paul in the above verses painfully reflect the reality of life: "We get knocked down, but we get up again and keep going."

How do you ever get over the loss of a little one or a spouse? The bottom line is that you will never get over it—but you can learn to live with the pain. Jesus Christ is here with us crying, holding, and comforting us in those moments of despair and weakness. And by living with the pain, you model for a lost and dying world the very life, death, and resurrection of Jesus Christ. He endured his pain so that we might have life. When we live with our pain, we allow Jesus Christ to shine through us to a dying world in pain without hope.

Reflections on Surviving the Loss of a Loved One

Twelve years have passed since that tragic day of May 7, 2000. Now that you know my story may I now share with you some of the things my family and I have learned while traveling the path of grief.

You have to make a choice

First, when you lose someone you love you have a choice to make. You can choose to live, or you can choose to stop living. This statement sounds very cold, but having personally walked the path of the grieving and ministering for thirty years to others who are grieving it appears that there are two basic responses to the loss of a loved one. One you choose to live. Somehow. Someway. In spite of all the pain, you continue to do what is necessary to keep going. Or you may choose to stop living. I know a woman in a church where I served as a part-time pastor who lost a son about twelve years ago. She has never been able to move on from that tragic loss. She is unable to work. She does not function in the community. She rarely gets out. She goes to her son's grave almost every day. She stays sick from living in constant and ongoing grief. She has chosen not to live. You have to make the choice: to live or to stop living.

It will be a difficult journey

Second, if you choose to continue on, there will still be many difficult days ahead. The waves of grief come upon you in mysterious ways and at mysterious times. You never know what may trigger the memory of that loved one who was lost. You need to give yourself permission to grieve anytime or anywhere. I have missed several May graduations where I have served as a college professor because of the graduation day's proximity to the anniversary of my son's death. When I am grieving I choose not to be around a lot of other people. College graduation is an important day in the life of a college student, but my well-being and the well-being of my family continues to be my first priority. There is nothing in this world that can prepare you for the loss of a close loved one like a spouse or a child. All the books, pamphlets, or blogs cannot prepare you for the difficulty of those who lose loved ones.

Seek help from others

Professional organizations. Please do not be afraid of seeking help with your grief. For those of you who have lost children, organizations like *Compassionate Friends* can be a great resource for processing your grief and loss. My wife and I only attended a few meetings of *Compassionate Friends* in Raleigh during the year after Jake's death, but it really helped me to know that so many other people were either going through the very same thing, or something very similar to what I had experienced. At my first meeting I was amazed at how many names I recognized from the news media of the past few years. Those tragic events with the loss of life at that point came to have real faces and became real families who were left behind.

Faith communities. Please do not withdraw from others and from the sense of community. Many people do not know how to assist you when you are in pain, but many people will want to help. Let others become part of your healing process. Though many people who are well intentioned will often say some inappropriate things like "heaven just needed another angel," or

"God was just saving your son from something worse," or "you'll learn someday why Jake needed to die." Be able to overlook these well-meaning but thoughtless comments and take the intent of the speaker and not the actual words to heart.

The churches I mentioned, Westfield Baptist Church in Dunn, North Carolina and the First Baptist Church of Buies Creek, North Carolina ministered to me and my family on a daily basis. They continue to hold a special place in our hearts today. I do not know what we would have done without such great communities of faith.

Friends who have also lost loved ones. I teach at a liberal arts college in East Tennessee best known for being a Division II Football powerhouse called Carson-Newman College. I have three great friends who have taught in my department with offices besides mine and across the hall from mine who have also lost children.

Don Garner had a college-aged son, Aaron, who died from injuries sustained in a car accident in Durham, North Carolina. Aaron died a year before Jake did. During that time I was teaching in the Raleigh-Durham area at Campbell University and I did my best to visit Don at the hospital at Duke University the week that his son Aaron lay dying in I. C. U. He has become a life-long friend and we often talk about our sons' untimely deaths and the impact that it has made on our lives.

Carolyn Blevins is now retired from Carson-Newman, but for the first four years of my work at C-N her office was just across the hall from mine. In August of 2004, while preparing for her mother-in-law's funeral the Blevins' realized that their adult daughter had not made it to the funeral home. Bill and Carolyn sent two of their sons across town to check on their daughter only to discover that she had been murdered.

David and Carol Crutchley lost their beautiful daughter and mother of their granddaughter just as the academic school year was commencing a few years ago.

The four of us on the hallway have been a source of strength and reinforcement. No one begins to understand the depth of pain and anguish you go through in the loss of a loved one unless you have walked a similar life of pain.

Be sensitive to the needs of other family members. Every member of my immediate family has "Jake" moments. We still have "Jake" days when we are just going to be sad. They are more frequent around the holidays and anniversary dates like Jake's birthday or the anniversary of his death. But these days can appear out of the blue and there is nothing you can do to control their appearance. At the recommendation of others my family has dedicated the word "bumble-bee" to describe this phenomenon. When we are together in the presence of others and we are having a "Jake" moment we incorporate the word "bumble-bee" into our conversation and our immediate family knows that the other family member is hurting. We all have committed to do what it takes to help politely provide a means of escape for that family member from that given social context. Sometimes it means leaving public dinners early. Sometimes it means leaving parties even before the party seems to have begun. Please do not try and ignore the grief that you are processing or feeling! If you do then it is more likely to resurface in unproductive ways rather than in being incorporated into the healing process. Be sensitive to the needs of your family members and plan ahead to best meet their individual needs for grief.

I had a younger brother who was stillborn on December 26, 1969. Every year my family knows that my mother is not to be disturbed on the day after Christmas. It is an annual time of mourning, reflection, and dealing with her loss in a personal way. We give my mother "her" space.

The Hope

I trust you have noticed I have not said a word about the resurrection, or about heaven. I do want to affirm that I have hope through faith in Christ and I look forward to a heavenly reunion with my dear sweet little Jake. I pray and believe that day will come soon enough. But I do not want to face my son on that day with the thought that I wasted a single day not living life to the fullest.

> [19]*The thought of my affliction and my homelessness is wormwood and gall!* [20] *My soul continually thinks of it and is bowed down within me.* [21]*But this I call to mind, and therefore I have hope;* [22]The steadfast love of the LORD never ceases, his mercies never

> come to an end; [23]*They are new every morning; great is your faithfulness* (Lam 3:19-23; *RSV*).

I would close these words with a prayer for every one of you who has lost a loved one. And I pray for every one of you who regularly ministers to those who are in pain, suffering from the loss of a loved one.

> *Dear God, Hear our cries of anguish. Remember us in our times of distress. Help us to rely upon your healing, your guidance, and your grace. Help us to navigate the course of our lives through the dark shadows of death's door. Enable us to live each day in courage and strength—knowing that you have neither forsaken or abandoned us, nor have you condemned us. Help us to count upon your understanding, because we know, you lost your son too! Amen.*

Notes

[1]Today We Buried a Child" was penned by Dr. Walter Shepherd Barge, Dean of the College of Arts and Sciences at Campbell University in May of 2000. Dean Barge presented these words to me following the funeral for Jake. This moving tribute is prominently displayed in a frame in our home. I would like to thank Sarah Barge, wife of the late Dr. Barge, for granting me permission to use these words as part of this chapter.

[2]"Living with the Pain" was first presented to the Campbell University Divinity School Chapel on November 6, 2001 and has been presented on many subsequent occasions including twice per request at the Community Life and Worship experience at Carson-Newman College.

[3]"Reflections on Surviving the Loss of a Loved One" was presented to the Trinity Baptist Church in Cordova, Tennessee in April, 2008 as a keynote address as part of a larger conference dealing with the loss of a child.

[4]C. S. Lewis, *The Problem of Pain* (New York: Collier Books, 1962), 26.

[5]Chad Walsh, "Afterword," in *A Grief Observed* (Toronto: Bantam Books, 1961), 126-127.

[6]*Ibid.*, 149.

[7]C. S. Lewis, *A Grief Observed* (Toronto: Bantam Books, 1961), 1.

[8]Richard Hipps, ed. *When a Child Dies: Stories of Survival and Hope* (Macon: Smyth & Helwys Press, 1996).

[9]Nicholas Wolterstorff, *Lament for a Son* (Grand Rapids: William B. Eerdmans Publishing Company, 1987).

[10]John R. Claypool, *Tracks of a Fellow Struggler* (New Orleans: Insight Press, 1995). *Revised Edition.*

Ministering to the Suffering: Pastoral Theology from the Book of Job

J. Randall O'Brien, Ph. D.
President and Professor
Carson-Newman College

THE FACE OF THE YOUNG BOY CAUGHT my attention. It seemed painfully out of place among the other pictures on the obituary page. His was the face of an angel, I thought. So peaceful. So innocent. So beautiful. Eleven years young. Gone. Beneath the haunting picture appeared these weeping words, "In Memoriam," from the family of the departed child:

> *Please don't ask us if we're over it yet. We'll never be over it. Please don't tell us he's in a better place. He isn't here with us. Please don't say at least he isn't suffering. I haven't understood why he had to suffer at all. Please, please don't tell us you know how we feel, unless you have lost a child. Please don't ask us if we feel better. Bereavement isn't a condition that clears up. Please don't tell us at least you had him for 11 years. What year would you choose for your child to die? Please don't tell us God never gives us more than we can bear. Please just say you are sorry. Please just*

say you remember Ryan. Please just let us talk about him. Please mention Ryan's name. Please just let us cry. Our hearts are broken, our home is empty. Son, we love and miss you so much. Only God knows.

Love, Mom, Dad, Sister, and all your animals

What is wrong with this "pastoral theology?" Absolutely nothing! Every word is sacred. Every word is a gift to caregivers everywhere.

Christian care-giving is a delicate art, which may be learned. Equal parts of sensitivity and wisdom are required. Most of us would confess that we never feel adequate to minister to the bereaved, or other grief-stricken persons. Painfully feeling our limitations, we rely upon prayer and the comforting presence of the Holy Spirit in our ministry to the suffering. We may also gain invaluable guidance for pastoral care to hurting persons by reading the biblical Book of Job, as well as literature on stages of grief and faith development.

The Story of Job

Tragically, bad things happen to good people in this world, even God's people. From Abel, (whose name means "wind or breath," symbolizing the fleeting nature of life) who falls victim to his brother, Cain (whose name means "spear") to Jesus, our sinless Savior (who is speared in a criminal's death on a bloody cross), the Bible clearly reveals that no one in this life is guaranteed an asylum from innocent suffering.

In the story of Job, God's favorite suffers the horrible fate of losing ten children to death, when he is told:

> *Your sons and daughters were eating and drinking wine in their eldest brother's house, and behold, a great wind came across the wilderness, and struck the four corners of the house, and it fell upon the young people, and they are dead.* (Job 1:18-19)

This unspeakable tragedy afflicts Job even though he is a "**blameless** and upright man, who fears God and turns away from evil" (1:8; 2:3). The LORD had proclaimed before Job's trial that, "There is **none like him** on earth" (1:8). Yet, Job would suffer horribly. The Adversary had challenged the LORD's assessment of Job inquiring cynically, "Does Job fear God for naught?" (1:9), meaning he contemptuously questioned the character of Job's faith. Disagreement leads to divine wager, which leads to trial. Thus the main plot of the story revolves around this central issue: does Job love God unconditionally, as the LORD believes? Or does Job love God for what he receives from God, as the Satan implies? The question is: Does Job love God or self? If he was to suffer, rather than enjoy prosperity and the good life, would he continue to worship God? Or, would he curse God to the face, as the Satan insists? (1: 10-11).

Job is certainly on trial. Perhaps it is also fair to say that the story of Job is not so much about suffering as it is about Job's relationship with God. Since Job is the story of every person, the storyteller intends to prompt the hearer, or reader, to ask, "What is the character of my relationship with God? Do I worship God regardless of circumstances?"

God had one Child without sin, but never one without suffering. Sooner or later we all suffer. Life is a fatal disease. Humans are 100% terminal. Some suffer at the hands of evil. Others suffer from natural causes. Some suffer at a young age. Others languish late in life. Psychologists tell us the greatest tragedy one might experience is the loss of a child. Parents do not expect to bury a child. Regardless of the child's age, no pain is greater than the death of one's child. Job lost ten children.

How are we to think when a crisis of innocent suffering strikes? How are we to talk to God, and about God, when we do not have all the answers? What do we say to a friend devastated by tragedy?

Remember that Job suffers innocently. If we miss this truth, we miss the central plot of the story, and several important lessons for living. We must remember that Job is described by the LORD as "blameless." Job is God's favorite. "There is none like him in all the Earth," the LORD declares. Yet, disease, death, and destruction visit Job's family as he loses his wealth, health, and children. How would Job respond? How would his relationship with God be affected?

Remember Job's friends, Eliphaz, Bildad, and Zophar, come to minister to him. As friends and caregivers they do some things right, but many things wrong, incurring the wrath of God. We can learn from their virtues, but also from their mistakes.

Job and his friends fiercely debate the nature of God (chapters 4-14), then argue viciously over the fate of the wicked (chapters 5-21). In steadfastly maintaining his own innocence while suffering, Job questions the justice of God. Job's friends, however, passionately defend divine justice and pronounce Job guilty of sin, which they insist is what brought punishment upon him. After all, the friends contend, we all get what we deserve. Not always, Job countered; not always. Who is right, Job or his friends?

Remember that the LORD speaks from the whirlwind at the close of the story. This speech is God's longest in the Bible. Ultimate lessons for living and ministering to the suffering await us in this story. For instance, is it okay, or wrong, for victims of ill fortune to question God?

Have you noticed that when bad things happen to good people, some well-meaning caregiver inevitably asserts, "we should not question the Lord; ours is not to ask 'why?'" Is counsel such as this kind healthy? Is it biblically sound? Jeremiah certainly asked, "Why?" Habakkuk asked, "Why?" So did the Psalmist. Job asked, "Why?" five times in chapter 3 alone. Even Jesus cried out from the cross, "My God, my God, why have you forsaken me?" (Matt 27: 46).

These authentic persons did not question God due to the absence of a personal relationship with their heavenly Father. On the contrary, it was precisely because they enjoyed such an intensely intimate relationship with their heavenly Father that each felt the freedom to express his true feelings. Honest questions belong in intimate relationships. The Book of Job encourages us to journey from acquaintance to intimacy with our God. Our Lord welcomes honest conversation, which is true prayer. If it were a sin to ask God, "Why?" our Savior would not be sinless.

Let us, then, examine the stages of faith for insight into various ways persons may legitimately respond to grief.

Stages of Faith

James Fowler's early work in faith development (*Stages of Faith*)[1] found six stages of faith in human development. Besides the first two, which pertain to infants and children, and the last, which is an exceedingly rare characteristic of exalted sainthood, the three basic adult stages of faith remain: **non-questioning, questioning, and conjunctive.**

The **first** of these is a devotional, non-critical stage, characterized by a naïve, obedient heart completely trusting of authority **external** to one's self. This stage of faith has been described as "the tyranny of the they." What "they" say is ultimately important. This outlook depicts a conformist approach to life. One in this mode of relating would neither dare question God, nor appreciate others doing so. Job's friends, Eliphaz, Bildad, and Zophar, and later, Elihu, stand firmly in this position.

The **second** of these three development phases describes a critical, examining, reflective season of relating to all others, or one characterized by an intellect which insists on thinking for itself. Authority is **internal** in this stage of faith; namely, a person in this category is given to critical reflection, even doubt, insisting on the right to think freely and boldly. Such a pilgrim no longer sees the world as black and white, but rather as complex. One in this phase feels the freedom to question God and extends the same permission to others. This dominant stage of faith represents Job.

The **third** stage, the **conjunctive** (meaning "to join together") stage of faith, brings a wedding of head and heart. A person in this relational stage desires "to make sense of it all," even though she is quite alive to paradox, contradiction, and uncertainty. The drive to re-submit, or "to come home," leads this person to make a life commitment amidst unresolved mysteries and complexities. At the end of the story, Job comes to this point.

One might think of the Prodigal Son as an example of one traveling through these three seasons of life. In the beginning he is content, devotional, and adoring of his father. Then he goes his own way, intent upon being his own person and doing things his way, while learning for himself. Later, he comes home to his father, ready to re-submit to his authority. The younger boy's journey correlates with Fowler's ideas on stages of faith (non-questioning, questioning, and, in essence, return).

The Swiss psychologist, Piaget, writing in *The Moral Judgment of the Child,*[2] argues that life's journey winds through the following stages of development: (1) We play by the rules, (2)

We make up our own rules, and (3) We return to the rules. The parallel to Fowler's work is striking.

Regardless how we label these three relational approaches, Job, like the Prodigal Son, moves through each successively. At the outset, in the first two chapters, he steadfastly refuses to question God, exclaiming:

> *Naked I came from my mother's womb and naked I shall return; the LORD giveth and the LORD taketh away; blessed be the name of the LORD.* (Job 1:21)

Then, beginning with chapter three in the book, Job becomes angry, verbalizing his rage bitterly as he "opened his mouth and cursed the day of his birth" (3:1). Repeatedly, Job demands answers from God, crying: "Why did I not die at birth, come forth from the womb and expire?" (3:11). Yet, in due time Job re-submits confessing:

> *I have uttered what I did not understand, things too wonderful for me .... I had heard of thee with the hearing of the ear, but now my eye sees thee . . . therefore I . . . repent in dust and ashes.* (Job 42: 5, 6)

Fowler's research and the biblical text of Job teach us, among other things, that it is natural to go through different stages of faith in times of deep grief and sustained periods of suffering. God created us that way. Of course, we may not wish to question God at all when innocent suffering strikes. On the other hand, we may long to scream out for answers. Caught in the grip of grief we may go through mood swings and various relational approaches. But such is the essence of being human. Why should we not feel the freedom to think our thoughts and feel our feelings, even express our deepest doubts to God, since God knows them anyway? Hopefully, our commitment to God remains rock-solid even though we may never receive all the answers we seek.

If there are stages of faith, are there also stages of grief? To state the question in another way: Are there predictable emotional responses to grief, which persons languishing in loss, and ministers to the grief-stricken, should anticipate?

Stages of Grief

Elisabeth Kubler-Ross's work in the area of death and dying (*On Death and Dying*)[3] merits mention here. Her research on the grieving process identifies five stages of grief: (1) Denial, (2) Anger, (3) Bargaining, (4) Depression, and (5) Acceptance.

These five stages, Kubler-Ross writes, are normal responses to loss. Their presence is predictable in the lives of the grief-stricken, and appear to be evident in the life and words of Job. Initially, it could be argued, Job does not question God because he is in shock and denial over the deaths of his ten children, followed by the loss of his estate and his health. "The LORD gave and the LORD has taken away," Job manages; "Blessed be the name of the LORD." (Job 1: 21). Soon, however, anger and depression surface in his harsh criticism of God and his desire to die. "Why did I not die at birth," Job cries, "For the arrows of the Almighty are in me" (3: 11; 6: 4). In time, Job accepts his terrible fortune, becomes a rebel who lays down his arms, and comes to terms with the reality of his existence saying, "I repent in dust and ashes" (42: 6).

Kubler-Ross and the Joban text show us that grief-work is not a singular emotional state. Rather, one who suffers loss should expect to experience a range of emotions. Friends and ministers should also anticipate sufferers being tossed about on emotional roller-coasters. "Everyone can master a grief but he who has it," Shakespeare observed in *Much Ado About Nothing* (Benedick in *Act III Scene 2*)[4] It is unrealistic to expect one assaulted by grief to maintain any one particular emotional response. Spiritual, theological, psychological, intellectual, and relational responses may all prove kaleidoscopic.

As previously mentioned, the Christian caregiver should grant to the grieving person the grace to speak honestly to God and to all others. The grace to express anger, doubt, fear, loneliness, unbelief, and betrayal is a therapeutic gift. Honest, intimate conversation enhances wellness. Let us remember our Savior's cry, "My God, my God, why have you forsaken me?" Does God ever forsake us? No! Do we sometimes feel forsaken? Perhaps. If so, it is okay to be honest and verbalize our harshest thoughts. Jesus did.

Lessons for Ministers and Other Caregivers

One of the most important lessons derived from Job, Fowler, and Kubler-Ross is that in the course of normal human development, certainly in the event of acute grief-work, it is normal, predictable, and acceptable to come to a time when hard questions are asked, when anger is expressed, when depression occurs, and when our deepest thoughts and rawest emotions rise to the surface and beg expression. Those among us who are most in touch with our humanity and our spirituality will embrace this grace and grant it to others.

A **second** lesson for Christian ministry, among many in the Book of Job, literally screams its message for readers of Job's story and especially for caregivers to those who are suffering. We must **never** make the mistake of believing, or implying, that were the faith of the victim great enough, suffering would be removed by God. This sort of theology is nonsense. The LORD pronounced Job **"blameless and upright,"** one who "feared God and turned away from evil," announcing "there is none like him on all the earth" (1:8). Yet, Job suffered horribly. Paul prayed three times to be healed, but God replied, "My grace is sufficient for you" (2 Cor. 12:9). Facing the cross Jesus prayed, "Father if it be Thy will, let this cup pass from my lips" (Matt. 26:39). Yet, he died on the cross. Was the faith of Job, Paul, and Jesus deficient?

Third, unlike Job's friends, we must never assume that one is guilty of some secret sin and therefore deserves the tragedy at hand. One of the major lessons the story of Job teaches is that we do **not** always get what we deserve. Bad things **do happen** to innocent people. The tendency to blame the victim is an unconscious attempt to control God. "As long as I am good, God will provide me an asylum from evil," one might think. Or,

"Since she is in this horrible predicament, she must have done something wrong to deserve such pain," one might reason. The roll call of martyred saints, prophets, and apostles throughout the ages might have something to say about this sort of theology. Yet, Eliphaz, Bildad, and Zophar all claimed that we do, in fact, reap what we sow. Without exception, they argue, the righteous are rewarded, while sinners suffer. But is such reasoning always the case in this life?

It is true that the Books of Deuteronomy, Proverbs, and all the Prophets stress a theology of just desserts, i.e., "we get what we deserve." The author of the Book of Job would not likely contend that such theology is incorrect, just incomplete. The teaching of Job strives to complete the biblical revelation on the subject of innocent suffering. All rules have exceptions. We do not **always** get what we deserve in this life. Alas, we learn slowly the real truth about life. Therefore, hundreds of years after Job lived, Jesus stressed again this important truth in the Sermon on the Mount. He taught that the "Father who is in heaven makes the sun rise on the evil and on the good, and sends rain on the just and on the unjust" (Matt 5:45). Christian caregivers should be less concerned about determining guilt, and more concerned about dispensing grace.

Fourth, loved ones who are hurting desire our presence, not our preaching. The gift to the broken-hearted is the gift of listening. "The road to the heart is the ear," Voltaire wrote, "The gift of silence is a grace."[5] As long as Job's friends sat with him and said nothing they ministered powerfully as comforters. What a beautiful example of tender pastoral care they provide at that point:

> *Now when Job's three friends heard of all this evil that had come upon him, they came each from his own place . . . . They made an appointment together to come to console with him and comfort him. And when they saw him from afar, they did not recognize him; and they raised their voices and wept; and they rent their robes and sprinkled dust upon their heads toward heaven. And they sat with him on the ground seven days and seven nights, and no one spoke a word to him, for they saw that his suffering was very great."* (Job 2: 11-13)

Now that example of presence is the way to minister! But sadly, the three friends open their mouths and trade grace for disgrace. Eliphaz proclaiming:

> *Think now, who ever perished that was innocent? Or where were the upright destroyed? As I have seen, those who plow iniquity and sow trouble reap the same. By the breath of God they perish. And by the blast of his anger they come to an end.* (Job 4: 7-9)

Bildad further exclaiming:

> *Does God pervert justice? Does the Almighty pervert what is right? If your children have sinned against him (God), he has delivered them in to the power of their transgression. If you would seek God . . . if you*

> *are pure and upright [he would] restore your righteous estate* (Job 8: 3-6).

Then Zophar pronounces,

> *Know then that God exacts of you less than your guilt deserves . . . An idiot will become intelligent when the foal of a wild donkey is born a man.*
> (Job 11: 6, 12).

Woe is me! When Job desperately needed salve, his "comforters" gave sermons, and bad ones at that! Job needed grace; instead he received nonsense. Grace is from God; nonsense is not.

Fifth, God yearns for honest, open, intimate expression of our genuine thoughts, feelings, questions, and doubts; therefore, no person may stand between God and another human, attempting to block such sacred, intimate conversation. Repeatedly, Job poured out his heart to God, albeit in seemingly blasphemous words, and repeatedly, his "comforters" berated him for his "heresy." Once he wailed, "From the city men groan and the souls of the wounded cry out; yet God pays no attention to their prayer" (24:12). Bildad responded, "How then can a man be righteous before God . . . much less man, who is a maggot" (25: 4, 6).

The willingness to talk outrageously to God may, in some situations, constitute true prayer. God desires honest communication, not hollow sounds from His people. When we rest in God's unconditional love and acceptance our large masks of piety and pretense fall away. Our defense mechanisms relax, and soon become obsolete. We become our real selves and express our honest thoughts to God, because we know we can trust God's grace and love. Fear gives way to faith. Conversation becomes communion. We journey from acquaintance to intimacy. Prayer and spiritual growth happen.

As the Book of Job draws to a close, the LORD roars to pious Eliphaz, "My wrath is kindled against you and your two friends: for you have not spoken of me (or perhaps, "to me") what is right, as my servant Job has" (42:7). The friends spoke **well *of* God**; Job raved **shockingly to God**. There is a huge difference between religion and a relationship. Guess which one our LORD prefers?

Sixth, Job is the only one in the story growing in maturation and in his relationship with God. The friends, who steadfastly refuse to question God, or even to allow it, fail to understand that doubt is not always the antithesis of faith; it may prove to be the cutting-edge of faith. Job's honest communication with God, however abrasive to others, ushers him into a deeper relationship with the LORD. In the end Job testifies, "I had heard of thee with the hearing of the ear, but now my eye sees thee." (42: 5). Job grew closer to His God, even though he never knew all of the story. None of us ever do. So the question becomes, "How are we going to talk about God and to God when we do not know the whole story of our trials?" Apparently, honesty is still the best policy.

The friends, smugly uttering their plastic platitudes, canned clichés, and syrupy, superficial spiritual-speak, met with severe reprimand from the LORD. Instead of being allowed to offer the usual one bull or goat sacrifice ordained for unintentional sin (Lev. 1-5), the miserable comforters are commanded by God to sacrifice **fourteen** animals, **then** ask Job to **pray** for them! "I will accept his prayer," God thunders, "not to deal with you according to your folly" (42: 8). Sadly, the friends have valued "beliefs over brother," "doctrine over decency," "law over love," and "religion over relationship." Big mistake!

Seventh, when the LORD at last answers Job out of the whirlwind at the story's end, the mystery of innocent suffering remains. What Churchill once said of Russia may be said of this eternally haunting question: "It is a mystery, inside a riddle, wrapped in an enigma."[6] Chesterton wrote, "The riddles of God are more satisfying than the solutions of man."[7] Good thing, because God gives no explanation to life's greatest riddle. Why do the innocent suffer? The writer of Deuteronomy testified, "The secret things belong to the Lord our God" (29: 29). Paul confessed, "We see through a glass dimly" (1 Cor. 13: 12). John Calvin (1509-1564) preached 159 sermons on Job. Divine incomprehensibility and inscrutability may well be Calvin's leading theme in his writing and preaching on Job.

The problem of innocent suffering remains a mystery. But that is okay. Mystery is a form of reverence for God. In essence, the LORD announces, "My answer is, there is no answer; not in this life."

To be sure, questioning is permissible, but mystery prevails. At the end of the day, "the just shall live by faith." There is something better than understanding God. It is trusting him.

Eighth, The LORD assures Job that God is far wiser than we, that the universe plays out by intelligent design, and that he is in ultimate control of the world, including chaos and evil, which are limited and temporal (38-41). Our song from childhood expresses this truth well: "He's got the whole world in His hands."

Ninth, despite Job's cynicism (articulated acidly centuries later by H. G. Wells when he opined, "Our God is an ever-absent help in our time of need.")[8] God is, in fact, present, not absent. God shows up. God speaks (38-42:8). What we learn from the story of Job is that God is often present most where he appears to be least there. Although we learn this truth from the story of Job, the reality is perfectly revealed at Calvary. God has never been anywhere quite like he was at Calvary; yet, no one thought he was present at all. In our own Joban-like sufferings and cross-experiences, as well as those of our loved ones, we will need to remember these realities and walk by faith, not sight. Emmanuel: God is Emmanuel (God with us).

Tenth, as we minister to others who suffer, let us be sure to remember the teaching of Jesus recorded in Matthew 25: whatever we do to each other, we do to God. Job's friends learned this truth the hard way. Inasmuch as we speak offensive words, or encouraging words, to those who suffer, we speak those same words to Christ.

Eleventh, the story of Job reveals that the suffering of the righteous is redemptive. The way of the cross leads home. God chooses to use righteous suffering to draw persons closer to Him and to each other. Job and Jesus provide powerful examples of how the suffering of the righteous and their intercession atones for the sins of others. Madam Guyon puts it well: "God gives us the cross. The cross gives us God."[9]

Twelfth, and finally, we learn from Job that life properly viewed can only be acknowledged as a gift from God. All is grace. "Who has given to me that I should repay him?"asks the LORD. "Whatever is under the whole heaven is mine" (42: 11). Job exchanges his old theology of a world founded upon justice for one founded upon grace. God cannot be guilty of injustice because he owes none of us anything. God owes none of us more than he has given us. Creation itself is grace. Life is a gift. Life is grace.

Thomas Merton once wrote that there is no middle ground between gratitude and ingratitude.[10] Either we will be grateful or we will be resentful. Attitudes of entitlement lead to bitter resentment when disappointment strikes. Those who are grateful for life and understand it as sheer grace, however, celebrate God's grace and goodness and the precious, fleeting gift of life and witness.

Conclusion

In ministering to others who suffer (and in seeking to find our way as well when grief strikes us) let us remember these twelve lessons from the Book of Job. As always, humility, honesty, grace, and love minister well in any setting. Our love, prayers, and presence, along with God's amazing sufficient grace, always minister far better to those who hurt than any insensitive, uninformed sermonizing (including the ideas which appear in this chapter).

None of us have all the answers in life. In the end, Job never says, "I see it all." Job says to the LORD, "My eyes see thee." And that is enough.

Notes

[1]James W. Fowler, *Stages of Faith: The Psychology of Human Development and the Quest for Meaning* (San Francisco: Harper & Row, 1981).

[2]Jean Piaget, *The Moral Judgment of the Child.* Translated by Marjorie Gabain (Glencoe, Ill: Free Press, 1948).

[3]Elisabeth Kubler-Ross, *On Death and Dying* (New York: MacMillan, 1969).

[4]William Shakespeare, "Much Ado About Nothing" in *The Complete Works of William Shakespeare*, eds. William Neilson and Charles J. Hill (Boston: Houghton Mifflin, 1942), 179-210.

[5]Voltaire, *Epitres 54*, a letter to a Prince of Prussia in 1738.

[6]Winston Churchill, BBC London Radio Broadcast, October 1, 1939.

[7]G. K. Chesterton, *The Book of Job: An Introduction* (London: S. Wellwood, 1907), xviii.

[8]H. G. Wells, *Experiment in Autobiography: Discoveries and Conclusions of a Very Ordinary Brain* (New York: MacMillan Company, 1984), 46.

[9]Jeanne Guyon, *Experiencing the Depths of Jesus Christ* in the *Library of Spiritual Classics.* vol 2 (Sargent, GA: SeedSowers, 1975), 38.

[10] Thomas Merton, *Thoughts in Solitude* (New York: Farrar, Straus and Giroux, 1999), 32.

Learning from Loss

Carolyn D. Blevins, M. A.
Associate Professor, Emerita
School of Religion, Carson-Newman College

"YOU NEVER KNOW WHEN YOU PUT YOUR feet on the floor in the morning what that day will bring." How many times have I said that over the years? When I put my feet on the floor on Saturday, August 28, 2004, I expected a full day. But I hardly knew what was coming. Soon relatives would arrive for the funeral and burial of my mother-in-law. My ninety-two year old mother who lived in a nearby retirement home planned to attend. My brother was coming from out-of-state to take her. An early morning call from the retirement home reported that Mother was hemorrhaging. Soon I was in the ER with her. My brother came to the ER instead of the retirement home. I dashed home to get dressed for the funeral and set out the food which church members brought for our extended family's lunch. Our three oldest children who lived out of town were home for the funeral. Our youngest daughter lived in town but had not yet come to the house. Her brothers were concerned and went to check on her while I made tea in the kitchen. Shortly the phone rang. My husband, Bill, answered it in another room.

The next thing I knew he was standing in the kitchen saying, "Carolyn, Kym is dead!" Those are the three most knee-buckling, heart-crushing words I have ever heard. I broke into loud sobs as he held me in his arms. No! No! No! That idea was totally unimaginable. Kym dead? Not Kym! She was only thirty-two years old. In fine health! This message could not be correct! I sobbed loudly and uncontrollably. Relatives came from the living room thinking that my mother must have died, and were shocked to learn that it was Kym.

Within minutes Bill and I were on our way to Kym's house, five minutes away. No parent wants to drive up to her child's home and see a fire truck, an ambulance and a police car, but that is what we saw. Policemen were on the front porch. Kym's death appeared to be a homicide! Her death was shocking enough, but murder? Who would want to kill Kym? And why? And what was the cause of death?

As time for Bill's mother's funeral approached, he concluded that there was no way we could emotionally go through the important ritual of visitation before the funeral. Ministers at our church and a close friend volunteered to go to the funeral home, greet those who came and explain why we would be there for the funeral but not for the visitation. Later that afternoon as we sat at the cemetery before her grave I could only think of doing this again very soon. My grieving for family deaths was already all mixed up and could not easily be sorted.

Returning home I realized that when I put my feet on the floor that morning I did not know that in addition to a funeral, I would be in the ER with my mother, and mourning the death of my daughter. Now we waited for the officers from the local sheriff's department and the TBI to come to our home and interview our family. What a day!

When Kym was fifteen months old a Northwest Orient 747 plane brought her from Seoul, Korea to be the fourth child in our family. Thirty-one years later she was taken from our arms but not our hearts. We will forever be grateful for those thirty-one years with her.

A parent's worst nightmare is losing a child. Parents expect to be buried by their children, not the other way around. I was on a journey of which I had never dreamed or for which I had never planned. I did not know how to make this journey of loss. I had so much to learn.

When my body is wounded, the wound is treated. Soon new tissue grows in the wounded area. Eventually new skin covers the previous wound. If the wound is deep, a scar remains. A lot of healing has occurred but the body is forever scarred. Over the next months and years after Kym's death I discovered that my wounded spirit would also heal. There was new growth in that deep wound. But the scar is there forever. In the grieving and healing process I learned so much. A couple of weeks after Kym's death I began making a list of the things I was learning as a result of this tragedy.

The jolt of loss

Death and divorce are two losses our family has experienced. There are many other losses in life's journey that bring genuine grief to a person: loss of health, job, home, relationships, etc. As painful as they are, each of these devastating jolts in our lives can bring new growth in deep wounds. Most of us, in the process of growing up, learn how to gain or acquire. We learn little if anything about how to deal with loss. In the last seven years I have learned so much about loss and have so much yet to learn. Perhaps sharing some of what I have learned so far will be helpful to others.

The depth of grief

Books on grief and loss became important companions on my journey of grief. Kathleen Brehony's book *After the Darkest Hour: How Suffering Begins the Journey to Wisdom* was especially helpful. Brehony said that life places many different kinds of loss in our path. These darkest hours can lead to wisdom if we open that door. She had my attention when she said, "Grief is so deep it has no bottom."[1]

"This is so hard." Those four words came out of my mouth repeatedly on the shoulder and in the arms of friends over the first days and weeks after Kym's death. I knew no other way to express how I felt. As the days wore on I found new words to explain my emotions: "I feel like I have been hit by a bomb, one that keeps on dropping." Grief did seem to have no bottom.

I discovered new depths of sadness. The sadness seemed to permeate every bone in my body, every muscle, every cell, every crevice in my brain. It wrapped around me and through me. Never had I experienced such deep sadness. As I was dealing with the new depths, I was also experiencing sudden waves of sadness, sometimes seeming to come out of nowhere, not expected or predicted. I could go from feeling pretty good to feeling enormously sad in mere seconds. I had no idea what caused the swing and I learned that nothing in particular was the cause. These swings were the experience of grief. I began to compare these waves of sadness to an ocean. At times I floated in calm waters, calm with numbness, sometimes with a strange and brief peace. Then a huge wave of raw emotion swelled up and knocked me off my feet. Or a medium wave came and left me tearful. Or an undertow carried me sadly back into the ocean of grief. As a person who was able to control myself rather well most of the time, the inability to control this powerful emotion was quite disconcerting.

The search for self

I kept finding new "me's". Some of them I liked. Some I did not. In the early stages I was so focused on my own grief that I was rude to sympathetic friends that I should have appreciated. How embarrassing! One of the surprises was my hibernation. I like to go, to see others, to be with others. Suddenly I only wanted to hide in my home. There was a reason. I broke into sobs so easily, I did not want to make others feel ill at ease or embarrass myself. So I hunkered down in my shell like a turtle who only stuck her head out occasionally. This me was not the self I had known.

Faith is vital for me and church is a source of strength and community. The week after my father died, I went to church for worship as usual. Worship was normal for me. But after our daughter's death there was no way I was going to church. I knew if I did, that seeing people who were singing hymns and hearing God's message would reduce me to sobs; not just tears, sobs! I would be a major distraction and I would be embarrassed. I stayed away. I would have never predicted that pattern about myself. About a month later I began to sneak into the balcony after church started, sit on a bench against the wall, quietly let the tears flow, and slip out during the final hymn. But it was two months before I returned to my normal pattern of worship. I discovered another self, a more fragile one, who needed some healing time to worship corporately again.

Anyone who knows me very well, knows that I am a person with strong opinions. To my surprise some of my strongest opinions were changed by my experience with loss. Take capital punishment, for instance. For two decades I team-taught a course in which we discussed capital punishment issues. Every time I said, "I do not believe in capital punishment. If people should not kill, neither should the state. I am sure, however, that if someone in my family is ever killed, I will want that person put to death as punishment. It is the job of the state to protect that person from my vengeance." I meant every word of that statement.

Dealing with a homicide in my own family has not caused me to change my basic opinion. I still do not believe in capital punishment. Killing a man would not restore the life of my daughter, so why take another life? That view was always my basic reasoning: taking the life of another person was not redemptive. My rationale, however, changed in a flash. The issue now was not about the futility of retribution, but about being a mother. The thought of being a part of an effort to take the life of another woman's child was totally unbearable to me. My grief was so deep, so overwhelming! How in the world could I want another woman, any other woman, to experience that depth of loss. If she did, what good would that do me? All it would do is give another mother agony. Please do not even talk to me about capital punishment. Motherhood means more to me than vengeance. That change in my rationale has really surprised me.

As a Christian who takes the teachings of Jesus seriously, I do believe in forgiveness. There have been times in my life when I struggled with forgiveness. In fact, there was a time that I could not honestly speak those words in the Lord's Prayer. Like some of the other teachings of Jesus, practicing forgiveness is difficult.

I wanted to forgive the man who stole our daughter's life because it was the Christian thing to do. But I could not. I talked to God about my struggle again and again: "God, I want to forgive because it is the Christian thing to do, but to be honest that is not motivating me right now. I am ashamed to admit it God, but I want to forgive right now for selfish reasons. I do not want to be a bitter woman the rest of my life. He took Kym's life. I do not want to let him control my emotions for the rest of my life. I am being selfish, God. I do not want bitterness to envelop me so I have to forgive and free myself. God, I thought I was a better Christian than this, but I am not. So there it is. For now help me to forgive—selfishly."

The discovery of self

I was ashamed of that prayer, but I prayed it dozens of times. It may be the most honest prayer I have ever uttered. The real me was coming out and she was not very pretty. But there she was. I could not change this tragedy in my life. The only thing I could change was me. And I had a lot of work to do.

Why do I share these personal stories? It is because they helped me learn something important about me and about those who grieve. Those who experience deep loss **can discover** themselves at a level previously hidden. They may not be as confident, as kind, or as outgoing as they had been. That is OK. They are on a journey. Each person who grieves a serious loss in her life will find her way back to a self with which she is comfortable. That person will then be more aware of his or her strengths and weaknesses. Those who grieve can discover a new self.

Others Taught Me the Ministry of Caring

In *The Worst Loss* Barbara Rosof said, "to heal and rebuild we need the help of other people . . . to listen to our story, appreciate the depth of our pain, assure us that we are not going crazy . . . who understand the magnitude of our loss and the size of the job we face, who respect our journey, no matter how halting or detoured."[2]

The role of listening

Listening is one of the greatest gifts one can give a person who has experienced loss. Listening is not always easy. The person who sincerely asks "how are you doing?" weeks and months later and stays long enough actually to listen, gives a precious gift. Whatever the loss, its effects do not disappear in a couple of weeks. It is so easy to return to our normal routine and forget the lasting impact on the other person of losing a job, losing a marriage, losing health, or losing a family member.

People, however, vary in their ability to listen. They have differing reasons for not wanting to listen. I do not know what all of those reasons are, but they are probably quite valid. Who knows what troubling situation is going on in their lives? One of those reasons may be that they simply do not want to hear any more about my troubles. Quickly I learned that all of us have limits to bearing other people's burdens.

One refreshingly honest woman told me that she did not ask how I was doing because she did not want to bring it up and hurt me. I explained that I hurt both when she brought it up and when she did not, because I hurt all the time. I assured her it was OK to ask. But she taught me something very important. Some folks do not volunteer to listen because they do not want to bring up my hurt.

The power of hugs

Not everyone is a good listener. But many people are good at giving hugs! In one hug at a time I discovered the power of hugs. When my world seemed shattered, two arms wrapped around my broken being, assured me that another person shared my sorrow. People reached out to hug me and I reached out to hug them. Some of these people I would not have dreamed of hugging before August 28th! Suddenly I cherished every hug I could get. In the weeks that followed I learned how important hugs are.

How many times have I wondered what to say to a person whose heart was broken over what life had tossed her? Now I know that my words may be helpful, but my hug conveys as much as my tongue. A bear hug, an arm around the shoulder, a half-hug, whatever a person is most comfortable with, says "I care" in a way that lovingly embraces a person whose hurt is deep. I heard the worst words I have ever heard and immediately I discovered the arms of Bill. Quickly other hugs followed. Hugs have continued for days, and even years. They are caring, healing hugs.

Hugs come in various forms. Caring voices on the other end of a telephone call send a verbal hug. Written hugs float off cards as the sender finds words to share the pain and loss. Emails quickly sent to say that someone remembers and cares are technological hugs. Flowers are hugs of beauty. A month after Kym's death, a friend came to our home, handing us a hot chicken pie and saying, "I brought you this because I know grieving is exhausting." She left behind a culinary hug for our family, as well as a profound truth about grieving.

Hugs build community. Kathleen Brehony said that in difficult times relationships of family and friends are like a container. They hold us together, enclosing us in a space filled with love and belonging. "Community is not a luxury. It's like air for us," she concluded.[3] Friends and family were our container, holding us together. The sense of love and belonging as expressed in the variety of hugs was indeed air for our family.

The question of time

On Mother's Day, nine months after our daughter's death, a beautiful hydrangea arrived from one of our son's long-time classmates. What a thoughtful and lovely gift! When I called her mother to ask for her address to thank her, I heard this story: Her daughter who lived in another state told her mother that she wanted to express her concern, but she had waited too long to do so. Her mother replied, "It is never too late." And I learned another lesson. There is no such thing as expressing sympathy too late. Whenever it comes, it is most welcome. And "late" often comes when the person experiencing loss thinks no one cares any more.

It is never too late for an expression of care: a card, a call, a flower, some food, or a visit. Grief does not go away. It is never too late to care for another person who has lost what cannot be replaced. There is no such thing as too late. In the past I have chastised myself for failing to express my care in a timely manner. Sometimes I just did nothing because I thought it was too late or I was embarrassed that I had waited too long. Now I know: It is never too late to let someone know that I care.

The issue of avoidance

Earlier I confessed my hibernation. When I decided to venture out to the store for the first time in three weeks, I was very anxious. I worried about who I might bump into, what I would say and if I would cry. Like many other parts of the grief journey, this venture taught me something valuable. I did run into four people who spoke to me. One said a quick "hi" and rushed on to the next aisle. Another spoke, asked how I was and rapidly moved on. A third person rounded a display, saw me, threw open her arms and gave me one of those cherished hugs. A cashier whom I did not know said she knew of our loss and wrapped me in one of those warm embraces.

This trip had not gone as I expected. Walking to my car I realized: my fear of seeing others was no greater than others' fear of seeing me! Anyone who chooses to go to a visitation, stands in a line, knowing he or she will come to the grieving family and say something to each person and/or hug them. That friend wants to say something or give a hug and comes to do so. But when a person rounds a display in a store and bumps into me, she is not prepared to see me or respond to me and is taken completely off guard. As I stayed home to avoid people, I now realize that some people would also want to avoid me. This was a two-way street. Later I learned from Barbara Rosof that my experience is common.[4] People are often uncomfortable around someone who is dealing with loss and in fact will avoid them if possible. Again I realized that in our culture we learn more about success than we do about loss. Many people, especially those who have yet to experience loss, simply do not know what to say, especially when caught off guard.

The problem of closure

One of the puzzling aspects of grief for me was what people meant when they used the word "closure." After a year, especially as the date of a trial kept being pushed into the future, people began to say they knew we would be glad to get closure. I heard a lot of care and concern in those words. But after a while I began to ask myself, what is closure? The more I pondered the question, the more uncertain I was about what is closure. The dictionary did not help. So I began to wrestle with the concept of closure, for I too had wished closure for others. What did I mean? What do they mean?

Is closure forgetting? Forgetting is not possible. Is it absence of pain? Escaping pain is not realistic. Is it putting the past behind you? The dictionary meanings of closure focus on shutting off. There is no doubt that in their compassion our friends would have wished we could shut off the painful past, close the door on those events, remove them from our thinking. Closing such a door is a very loving wish for a hurting friend. But all of us, my friends and I, know that such a wish will not happen. Well, is it getting on with your life? I suppose this idea is a part of what we mean. Is it getting answers to the myriad of questions? Perhaps this is what closure means. Is it getting justice? Maybe it is. Is closure really possible? I began to wonder.

Kathleen O'Hara was helpful when I found these words, " . . . you are still grieving and, as much as you and everyone else would like to achieve closure, you cannot. . . . There is no closure. . . . People will insist we have closure, because they think it will be better for us and for them."[5]

When I hear someone say they want closure for our family, I do not try to figure out what they mean. I assume that they are wishing the best for us. As Ashley Davis Prend says: "Grieving is not a short-term process; it's not even a long-term process; it's a lifelong process . . . [it] does not have a final event built into it . . . grievers [who transcend] come to recognize the loss as a watershed event in their lives, as a meaningful life turning point."[6]

The significance of remembering

One of the most important gifts I have received from friends during this journey is what they have taught me about remembering. Any time someone mentions Kym's name, shares a memory of her, or sends a photo of her, it makes my day. That kind act lets me know that Kym is not forgotten by others. Remembering is such a gift. Especially is that true as her birthday or the anniversary of her death rolls around. When I get an email, phone call, card, or flowers on those days, I have one of those virtual hugs that tells me a friend remembers my loss. Friends who have remembered us at those times have taught me what a ministry remembering is to those who have experienced loss.

In loss, God has many faces

Where was God in this journey of grief? God was everywhere. God was in my hours of deep sadness; in my sobs; in my struggles to live as Christ taught; in the compassionate hugs; in the thoughtful cards; in the comforting foods; and in the acts of remembering. God has had many faces in my journey of grief.

The importance of forgiveness

God's major task with me was in the area of forgiveness. As mentioned earlier, my struggle with forgiveness began very early in my journey of grief. As a Christian, I do believe in forgiveness. But believing in it and practicing it are not the same. As I began to climb out of my pit of numbness, I realized I had to deal with forgiveness. As a person who takes the teachings of Jesus seriously I knew that I should forgive. But **should** and **would** were two very different paths. To be honest, I quickly ditched the idea that I would forgive because I am a Christian. My motive to work on forgiveness was not nearly so noble.

Selfishness drove my pursuit of forgiveness. I was not proud of this attitude of self-centeredness. I wanted to forgive because I believe as a Christian that it was the right attitude to have. But down deep I knew that I really wanted to forgive to be free of hate and anger. As C. S. Lewis said: "Everyone says that forgiveness is a lovely idea, until they have something to forgive."[7] That lovely idea did not sound so lovely to me. How could I be lovely in the midst of such horror? All of the bitterness and anger my body, mind, and soul could express would never bring Kym back. So what was its value? I wanted to live a life of as much peace as I could get. In order to do so, I had to forgive. For my sake, I had to forgive. If I wanted peace, there was no other option. Whether or not I forgave the person who took Kym's life would impact every day I lived and might have absolutely no impact at all on her killer. So if I did not forgive, I would pay the heaviest penalty.

Coming to such a conclusion added another kind of pain, for I wanted to think that I would do what a Christian should do. But I was choosing this path because it made me feel better. I was not proud of that motive. It was not the image of myself I wanted to have. But there it was. I admitted to myself that this motive was the best I could do at the time. Perhaps later I could be noble.

Imagine my relief months later when I read in Lewis Smedes, *The Art of Forgiving,*[8] that forgiveness is for oneself. In fact forgiveness is turning loose or letting go of those harsh feelings that imprison us. Books on forgiveness began to line my shelf. As I read I learned so much more about forgiveness. Forgiving another does not mean you are condoning or excusing what he or she does. It does not necessarily lead to reconciliation with that person. Forgiving certainly does not relieve the other person of the responsibility for dealing with the brokenness she or he has caused. Forgiveness does not mean forgetting. Coming to terms with these realities was very crucial. Sorting out what forgiveness was and was not relieved me of some of my misconceptions about it.

The benefits of forgiving

Revenge, bitterness, anger, and hatred would poison the very core of my being. If I could forgive, I would push those destructive feelings out, leaving room for more healthy feelings. I want peace. Bitterness and peace cannot live in the same house. The gift of turning loose of those hateful feelings was peace.

The challenge of forgiving

I have learned that it feels so much better to forgive than it does to refuse to do so. Jesus taught us to forgive because he knew it was best for the offended as well as the offender. To be forgiven is grace. To **be able** to forgive is grace also. A key resource in my journey of forgiveness was Philip Yancey's *What's So Amazing About Grace.*[9] Yancey challenged me to know grace at a new level.

The need for strength

The night of the memorial service for our daughter, one of our friends slipped a small bag into my husband's hand. When we got home we discovered she had given us a prescription for healing: a collection of prayers based on scripture passages, tightly rolled and inserted into old prescription bottles. Each passage had our names inserted. Each day we began the day by unrolling one and reading it together. When we read a prayer such as "Lord, we ask for peace for Carolyn and Bill; your peace, not the world's version. Comfort their hearts when they are troubled or fearful (John 14:27)." We indeed saw the face of God through a friend with old prescription bottles.

A few weeks later a friend asked, "What do you pray for?" Without a pause I said, "Strength and peace." Strength was essential to make this journey that was totally foreign to me. I realized immediately that I needed boat loads of strength. In fact, I did not just need strength, I needed strengths: many and a variety of them. God and I had a big job cut out for me!

My spirit needed strength. Not for one minute did I believe that God wanted someone to take the life of our daughter. At these times in the human experience I believe God is grieved also. My faith in God was unshakeable, even in this devastating moment of my life. What that faith meant in this time of crisis, however, confronted me with new challenges: How will this experience shape my faith? How does my faith instruct my response to grief? As a Christian, how do I respond to the person who has murdered our daughter, who has violated our whole family? How does my faith instruct my emotions of anger, pain, uncertainty, loss, and agony? How do I sing the hymns of faith with new confidence? To this day tears roll down my cheeks when I sing "Great is Thy Faithfulness" and come to the words "Strength for today and bright hope for tomorrow" for that continues to be my prayer.

The prayer for peace

"What do you pray for?" my friend asked. "Strength and peace," I replied. "Which do you want most?" Without batting an eye I said, "Peace." As much as I wanted and needed strength, more than anything else I craved peace. I needed peace, abundant peace. Being captive to the angry feelings associated with those horrible facts could easily lead me into a life time of bitterness. One thing I knew for sure: I did not want to live the rest of my life in bitterness, a person who lived in anger. I had to have peace in order to avoid becoming an emotional cripple.

With God's help I would live in peace; but it was going to take a lot of work on God's part and on mine. So I talked to God about wanting peace, talked to God about what peace could bring to my life, talked to God about how hard it was to deal with my anger, talked to God about my stabbing pain, about the depth of loss I felt, and begged for peace.

Right away I realized that God would not give me peace **unless** I was willing to work on it myself. Begging was not adequate. I had to work with God on this peace-seeking task.

Peace would not come if I prayed for it and then refused to make any effort on my part. God and I were partners in this effort and I had to be a willing receptacle for this gift, this grace of peace. My neighbor left a post-it note with Psalm 34:18 written on it: "The Lord is near to the broken-hearted." I stuck it on the fridge to remind me of the source of genuine peace.

A quotation from an unknown source was so helpful that I jotted it down and put it on my desk so that I saw it every day: "What might have been does not exist, so don't go there." I would not find peace if I focused entirely on what might have been, and that was so very tempting. It was so easy to dream painfully of what Kym's life would have been had she lived more than thirty-two years. My grief and the loss I felt centered on all that was lost for her and for us. But those "might have beens" did not exist and would not. Soon I learned that I would "go there" often and grieve the "might have beens" and that was OK; it was part of remembering Kym. But I also learned that to have peace I could not stay there. Peace would come when I came to terms with what has been and began moving forward toward what could be. This work was what I had to do for myself.

Devotional material relating to grieving pointed me to readings from the scriptures and from religious classics that brought the assurance of God's presence on this journey to peace. Lines from a familiar hymn[10] became my prayer:

Drop thy still dews of quietness
Till all my strivings cease

Take from my soul the strain and stress
And let my ordered life confess
The beauty of thy peace.

Many mornings I drove to work singing those words. They tended to settle me.

The crucial nature of gratitude

From the first day of this tragedy I realized that even in the midst of crisis we had some things for which to be grateful. Within a few weeks I began to make a list of those things. I could wallow in pity and at times I was up to my neck in a pit of pity. But that pit is an ugly place to dwell. Going back to read my thankful list helped me to climb out of that pit. I could also focus on where I found gratitude. Would I wallow in pity over the years Kym would not live or would I bathe in the memories of the thirty-two years she did live? Those alternatives were MY choices. One choice would keep me in turmoil. The other could lead me to peace. If God gave me peace I had to be ready to receive it. Some days I did not want it. Increasingly, however, I yearned for it and the freedom from anger that peace brought.

Peace is work. Peace is gift. Peace is a continuing journey, not a destination. Some days I have more peace than others. Our August Saturday morning was terribly and horribly broken. But the song "Morning Has Broken" sung at the memorial service for Kym pointed us to hope. "Praise every morning God's re-creation of the new day."

Conclusion

Not for one moment did I question God's love and care through this loss. Walking this journey without that divine presence was for me totally unthinkable. But knowing how to forgive and how to have peace was hard. It took a lot of talking to God to deal with my attitudes.

Walking this journey of loss without God is unimaginable to me. For I have seen the face of God in so many ways. In my personal struggles, I have experienced God while coping with my fragile emotions, while struggling with forgiveness and while seeking peace. In varied ways others have ministered to us: in their hugs, their cards, their calls and their visits; and also in the food, the flowers, the emails, the scripture and the books. These were the hands and voices of God at work in our community. They were the healing agents of God.

Loss pushed me to grow personally and spiritually. Loss taught me to appreciate the ministry of caring and remembering. Loss taught me so much about God, the divine Presence, the patient Healer. God help me to continue to be a willing learner.

"And remember, I am with you always . . . ." (Matt. 28:20)

Notes

[1]Kathleen A. Brehony, *After the Darkest Hour: How Suffering Begins the Journey to Wisdom* (New York: Henry Holt & Co., 2001), 156.

[2]Barbara D. Rosof, *The Worst Loss: How Families Heal from the Death of a Child,* (New York: Henry Holt & Co., 1994), 140.

[3]Brehony, 211.

[4]Rosof, 241.

[5]Kathleen O'Hara, *A Grief Like No Other: Surviving the Violent Death of Someone You Love,* (New York: Marlowe & Co., 2006), 120.

[6]Ashley Davis Prend, *Transcending Loss: Understanding the Lifelong Impact of Grief and How to Make It Meaningful,* (New York: Berkley Books, 1997), xv, 55, 85.

[7]As quoted in Brehony, *After the Darkest Hour*, 185.

[8]Lewis B. Smedes, *The Art of Forgiving* (New York: Ballantine, 1996).

[9]Philip Yancey, *What's So Amazing about Grace* (Grand Rapids, Michigan: Zondervan, 1998).

[10]John Greenleaf Whittier, 1872. From *Baptist Hymnal*, 1975 (Nashville: Broadman Press, 1975), "Dear Lord and Father of Mankind," hymn number 270.

Reflecting on Death and Grief: Perspectives for Ministry from the Gospel of John

Gerald L. Borchert, Ph.D., LL.B.
Senior Professor, School of Religion
Carson-Newman College

ANYONE WHO HAS BEEN A PASTOR, a hospital chaplain, a member of the healing professions, or a person engaged in hospice ministries knows the reality of death and grief. Indeed, as a former dean of two theological schools, I worked hand in glove with hospital administrators to deal with grief in an area where few people might suspect it would be evident. But that area was with nurses who were assigned to departments with terminally ill patients. We discovered in a number of cases that after a long period of hospitalization, relatives of such terminally ill people might adjust to the approaching death of loved ones and be ready to move forward with their lives, but at that point the nurses seemed to take up the grieving process. Many health care people and especially care-giving nurses are normally trained to help patients with the hope of aiding their recovery but they are oft not given adequate instruction and training in facing the stern reality of death and its impact on the care-giver's human psyche! And what can be said of health care people often happens with ministers as well.

The Harshness of Death

Death and human mortality are facts of life, yet humans would often rather paint over the cold reality of death with expressions like "crossing the bar" or "passing" than use stone-wrenching words like "died" and "dead." There is a brutal sense of emptiness and loneliness that sets in when the heart of a loved one stops beating and the breath which God gave to a partner, parent, child or friend (cf. Gen 2:7) ceases to be a *nephesh haya* (living being). The magnificent bouquets of flowers that often adorn beautiful caskets hardly compensate for the coldness of the body contained therein. Accordingly, giving a loved one a final farewell seems the least humans can do before that loved one is locked in the burial box, lowered into the ground and covered with dirt or cremated with the ashes being appropriately buried, stored or otherwise handled.

Having worked in a graveyard, I can tell you, it was an unforgettable experience. Digging up bones of those who had been entombed earlier so as to provide additional room for another body to be buried in the same plot helps one to realize very clearly the harsh reality of death. To see blond hair that had form one moment and then in the next moment witness it completely disintegrate into dust when it hits the air leaves a lasting impression of form without substance. It is a striking testimony to the nature of our human frailty.

Human Inclinations and Christian Clues

Preservation of the present reality is the wrenching desire of most humans but time moves on like the eerie drumbeat of a death march. Preserving bodies may be a human inclination but preservation of the body is hardly the message of the New Testament. Paul reminds us that the Christian view is "resurrection." Clearly, the Creator of the universe is hardly worried about preserving the elements of the body in order to provide a new body or a new instrument of expression for the self in the heavenly reality. Indeed, Paul contends with the Corinthians that what is sown in corruptible mortality will be raised and totally transformed into a new immortal reality which is totally different than the nature of human flesh (1 Cor 15:35-50).[1] One of the most interesting experiences for Christian travelers is to visit an early or medieval monastery such as St. Catherine's in the Sinai or the rock-pinnacle institutions at Meteora in central Greece. In those monasteries the monks gathered the bones of former colleagues and placed all the skulls together and the various other bones together in different containment rooms. The purpose in so doing was to witness to the world the unity of the community. Moreover, they firmly believed that even though their bones were merged in death, God knew who they were in life. Their witness concerning the enduring importance of Christian community was far more important to them than the self-centered individualism that marks the nature of much of western Christianity.

In reflecting on this fact, even given our propensity as westerners to focus on individualism, it is probably in facing death that we as humans recognize most clearly the commonality we share as mortals. And it is in sharing the grief of others that we often experience new and powerful senses of bonding. This recognition of commonality should be most evident among Christians who not only share mortality with all other humans but also share with other Christians the common hope that new life in Christ offers to us as mere mortals. Indeed, in spite of our frail mortality, hopefully "Christians"—who have this new life that comes from Jesus Christ—should even in death be able to provide for others a glimpse of the reality of life beyond the grave. Now being a Christian does not remove us from pain and suffering or the wrenching nature of losing the companionship of others who have been significant to us in this life. But it should provide us with a vision of the loving God who ultimately will wipe away all the tears from our eyes and it ought to supply us with a picture of the new era that will soon dawn when not only mourning will cease and pain will be removed but the great enemy death itself will be destroyed for ever (cf. Rev 21:4).[2]

Discovering this vision provides Christians with a significant resource for ministering to those who have been wrestling with death or have experienced the death of a loved one and who are encompassed with grief.

Some Reflections on Ministering to the Grieving from the Gospel of John

With these opening comments in mind, it is imperative to reflect on the insights that are offered to us in the New Testament. Given the limitations of time and space, however, I turn briefly to review a couple of selected texts from the Gospel of John which I believe can suggest some important perspectives for our understanding of grief and the task of Christian ministry with respect to death and dying.

Reflecting on John 11: the death of Lazarus[3]

The story of Lazarus offers some intriguing perspectives on the manner in which religious people often handle death and grief. The death of Lazarus was from the viewpoint of the sisters of Lazarus a major loss. In the ancient world which did not have the advantage of life insurance and Social Security, the death of the man of the house was viewed as a major economic concern. Furthermore, the text tells us that even Jesus regarded Lazarus as a special friend (cf. John 11:3). But in the pattern of Jesus who constantly seemed to upset the religious establishment by doing his healing on Sabbaths, here he postponed returning to the south and Lazarus's illness for several days, merely indicating that the illness was not a problem for him and that God would be glorified in the situation (11:4).

When later Jesus finally decided to go to Bethany, the disciples were troubled because they knew that the south was not a friendly place; besides, if Lazarus was not really ill and just "sleeping," he would certainly wake up. But in this case Jesus used "sleep" in the Old Testament sense as a euphemism for "death" (11:14). That realization brought fear to the minds of the disciples who focused more on the power of the world than on the presence of the Son of God. Nevertheless, the journey south took place.

As Jesus and the disciples neared Jerusalem, Martha arose from among the mourners and finding Jesus she bemoaned the fact that **"if only"** he had been present, her brother would not have died (11:21). Yet in good religious fashion, she added that God could do anything through Jesus (11:22). According to popular theory at the time, however, death by the third day was final because by that time any possibility of the person's spirit hovering near the tomb had gone and bodily deterioration had already taken place. Therefore, when Jesus indicated that her brother would rise and that Jesus was "the resurrection and the life," Martha responded that she knew good Pharisaic Jewish theology and that her brother would certainly rise at the end of time (11:23-25), yet from her point of view the life of her brother had now gone. Nevertheless, she still could make a great confession about belief in Jesus (11:27), even though her words did not connect to life at that point. Mary followed with a similar "if only" and the accompanying mourners when they saw Jesus' sorrowful reaction queried why the miracle worker could not have **"kept"** Lazarus "from dying." Of course, from their perspective, it was now also too late (11:35-36).

The rest of the story is a testimony about the fact that Jesus is not powerless in the face of death. Moreover, tombs and dead bodies are no hindrance to the power of God. But the point in using this story for our purposes here reminds us of several important matters:

The overwhelming nature of death. The world of death and evil often seems to be so overwhelming that the power of God appears to be helpless in the face of such a shattering human reality. Like Thomas, we may give up hope that God is able to handle our situations. Sometimes it seems that God's hands are tied and that the divine lacks power to intervene. Death, the last enemy (cf. 1 Cor 15:26; Rev 20:14), often seems to be omnipotent and evil may likewise appear to be overpowering. But Christians must never give up on the power of God even when they are in the throes of grief and when despair seems to be all encompassing.

The blinding power of grief. Death and grieving can easily blind us to the reality of God's presence in our midst with the result that we can fail to recognize the loving arms of God in Christ Jesus and the promise that he will be with us to the end of time (Matt 28:20), especially when it seems as though we are all alone and abandoned. In such times we may recite clichés that we learned in church or Sunday School, like Martha, but clichés are no substitute for sensing the presence of the living God. Nevertheless, in times of grief and great turmoil when God seems to be remote, it is important to remember that we need to offer the real presence of the faith community to the bereaved as the visible arms of the loving Jesus. Such support and comfort are crucial in times of anguish. God knew we needed one another and that is one important reason why God gave Christians the church.

The helplessness of wish-thinking. The words "if only" express a sense of human helplessness, regret and a longing to reverse the reality which has come to be. They are words of wistfulness and wish-thinking which we all tend to use as we experience and reflect on the troubling realities of life. They are realities the likes of which we do not want or the debilitating situations from which we cannot seem to escape or presently extricate ourselves. In the midst of our "if only" periods it is imperative to remember that while God is not in the habit of reversing our periods of grief, as in the case of Lazarus or of restoring our losses in the situations that seem to overwhelm us, God is nevertheless present in the model of Jesus and in the presence of the Holy Spirit to help us in finding a genuine way out of our entombing situations. Moreover, God's assistance is there whether in times of temptation or in periods of grief (1 Cor 10:13). It may take time to recover from our devastating experiences and it may be a very painful journey out of our bogs of life, but God understands each time we cry "if only." Yet the loving Lord will lead us step by step to a resolution of our traumatic pains.

Reflecting on John 14 to 16: the "departure" of Jesus and the coming Paraclete.[4]

As I have detailed in my commentary, the chapters briefly discussed here form the two central rings of the Farewell Cycle in the Gospel of John and deal with Jesus' counseling to his disciples as they were stricken with grief over his forthcoming death or "departure." Some of the verses in this section are often quoted at funerals and when pondered, they provide an excellent basis for gaining from Jesus some further dominical perspectives on grief. Perhaps some concerted reflection on these verses can therefore offer additional insights into the way Christians should approach the issues of death and grieving.

Considering the departure. The section begins with a carefully nuanced imperative for the disciples not to allow their hearts to be troubled at the departure of Jesus (14:1). The reason for Jesus offering such consolation is that human existence should not be viewed as the conclusion to authentic life. Jesus confidently sought to assure his followers that something greater can await them when this stage of existence comes to an end for humans.

Jesus himself considered that his role upon death was to prepare a future setting for his followers. The vivid translation at 14:2 of "many mansions" in the King James Version rather than mere "rooms," however, has led to all sorts of speculations concerning the Christian's inheritance in heaven. When that idea is joined to the vision of heaven where the streets of the holy city are made of an unearthly transparent gold (Rev 21:21), the stage is set for imagining that the believer's inheritance will be one that is rich and wealthy beyond all human imagination. That our future in Christ will be beyond imagination is undoubtedly correct but that it should be conceived in terms of human wealth is a far too mundane or earthly conception. The point of this introduction to the discussion on the Lord's departure is that Jesus was preparing a setting for his followers where they would find their fulfillment in being **with their Lord** (cf. 14:3).

But this announcement of Jesus' departure raised all sorts of questions on the part of the disciples much like the loss of a loved one raises all sorts of questions on the part of humans even today. "What does it all mean?" and "What is going to happen to me now?" are frequent queries that are uttered by the bereaved. Thomas, for example, asked a very human question when he could not conceive of where Jesus was going. Imagining that Jesus was departing on some sort of trip, he asked Jesus for "the way"—map or a "trip-tick"—so that he might be able to follow. But when Jesus responded that HE was the map to the Father, Philip made an additional naive request to see the Father and he would be satisfied. Little did he realize that he was asking for the impossible unless he wished his own death (14:8; cf. John 1:18; Exod 33:20).

Death or earthly departure raises many questions for those who suffer the loss of a loved one. Jesus' answer reminds one of a caring parent or teacher who seeks to lead a child to some new understanding. Kindhearted patience on the part of those who seek to minister and comfort the bereaved is an important lesson that we can learn from Jesus. Numerous questions come not only about a bereaved person's future but there are also questions of "Why?" which are normally there, even when they are not expressed orally. We will probably not be able to answer many of those questions, but answering those questions is not as important as providing a sense of personal presence for those in such circumstances. And that example is also in this text of John.

Jesus did go further with his followers who were feeling "abandoned" (John 14:18) and he offered them (and all of us) a new understanding of comfort. That comfort came in the form of providing the continuing presence of "**another**" (*allon*) companion.[5] That companion would be with them and would function as God's presence in place of Jesus (14:16). That companion, the Paraclete (*parakletos*) - which is translated in many ways including "comforter" or "counselor" - is available to every Christian. Accordingly, those who are in the midst of grief (and all of us) should not forget that God, the Father, who suffered when his Son went to the cross, understands intimately the nature of death and grief. In divine wisdom, the biblical God, who recognizes our human need for companionship, has with the Son sent the Holy Spirit to comfort and direct us who mourn and need consolation (15:26).

Recognizing the roles of the Paraclete in the face of grief. To recognize the multiple roles of this Paraclete – Holy Spirit – is therefore crucial for all those who would seek direction from the Godhead not only in times of pain and suffering but equally throughout all of life. In **five specific texts** in this section of John, Jesus beautifully enumerates those roles of the Holy Spirit for all who would take the time to study and reflect on them. While they are not all encompassing, they provide some marvelous insights into God's concern and care for us as mere mortals. Briefly I would draw your attention to these roles as follows:

Facing abandonment. Jesus indicated that those who follow his ways will have the Spirit of Truth not only "with" (*para*) them as Jesus was with them, but will also have this living and loving truthful one abiding "in" (*en*) them (14:17).[6] As a result, they should realize that they are NOT alone or "abandoned" but that in the Holy Spirit, Jesus actually comes to them (14:18). God's presence is with us (cf. Matt 28:20) at all times and in all circumstances even when such presence may seem to us to be very remote. We are **never** abandoned! Those, who have lost a loved one in death or divorce, know the debilitating feeling of abandonment that comes in such circumstances. It is at times like these that Jesus wanted us to recognize that we are never alone.

Forgetting who we are and needing peace. Even though we may become entangled in grief or seemly lose our footing and forget Christ's loving instructions to us, God has given us the Paraclete–the Spirit–to remind us of the ways and instructions of Christ (14:26). To forget is human, especially when we are encompassed with grief. To understand that our God knows that we forget and has sent the Holy Spirit to remind us in the midst of our human frailties about the ways of Jesus can be a great support and comfort to us. One of the painful experiences that humans encounter is to watch a loved one degenerate with the feared Alzheimer's disease so that the loved one does not seem even to recognize them any more. It is like a living death.

Yet in the midst of our anxieties and grief Christ speaks a word of consolation to his followers. His message is "Peace, I leave with you" (14:27). Our task as Christians who seek to help or minister to others in the face of such crises is to remind them that Christ has a consoling word of "peace" for them. That peace is far more real than comes from all the world's attempts at dealing with death and grief. But Christians can also provide an important aspect of needed companionship for those who are bogged down with the traumas of death, grief and turmoil. Nevertheless, it is the Holy Spirit acting through Christians that actually provides the genuine sense of peace. That peace can therefore be exemplified powerfully in the community of faith and inspire others to look to the living Lord, as Paul and Peter advise, for the true peace comes from God which can overcome all the worries and concerns of life (Phil 4:7; 1 Pet 5:7).

Becoming overwhelmed. Jesus will never abandon his followers. When our troubles and pains become overwhelming, however, like the disciples who abandoned Jesus at his arrest, trial and the cross, we can easily be tempted to abandon Jesus (16:32). But Jesus understands our frailties and has given us the Paraclete to be our internal witness to God's authentic, caring nature (15:26). Moreover, the Spirit's caring presence is intended to keep us from becoming a scandal ("falling away," 16:1). The Lord, of course, truly understands our outbursts of anger and our anguish during our times of loss when we feel completely abandoned and he has provided a personal resource to assist us in such times. God actually can handle our fear, our anger and our outrage, even when it is directed at the Lord Indeed, God in Christ has shown us by example how he related to his fallible disciples when they abandoned him. Do not think that God is unable to deal with human reactions. In seeking to help others, we, as mere humans, may become unhinged by such reactions of people who have experienced loss, but please remember that God is not a frail human. To express this idea in anthropomorphic terms, we might say: God has big shoulders and God can take our tirades.

Seeming to be useless. Jesus next said something that is almost unbelievable. He told his disciples that even though they were very frail, he would use them for his purposes in touching the rest of humanity through the work of the Paraclete. Is it really possible, even in our weakness and frailty, that God could use us to extend the gospel? The answer is a resounding "YES!" How can such a phenomenon be true? The answer is that divine transformation of others does not depend on us. We are merely agents of God; God is the actor. Anyone who is worthy of ministry, no matter how difficult or easy the situation may be, knows that transforming ministry is the work of God and not of mortal effort. Those in ministry, no matter how successful or impoverished their work may seem to be and who misunderstand this fact, have not yet learned the real secret of ministry.

In this fourth passage (16:7-11), what Jesus was telling his disciples is that through the presence of the Holy Spirit, God was and is at work in everything his followers are doing. The meaning of this text then is that in the coming of the Paraclete, the Holy Spirit would be using Christ's agents (followers) in engendering human reactions to Christ. Christians, by the very way they live, may seem to others to be following a set of rules, but rules are not what Christianity is all about. Christianity is about living with Christ. So, if Christians really live with the living Christ, then their lives will provide a standard for others to see their disobedience or "sin" against God. When others recognize that God does have a standard, they are confronted with the true nature of "righteousness." The result is that others are then faced with the reality of "judgment," when they compare their own lives with the standards of God (16:8-9).

But how does such an argument apply to those who are in grief? The answer to that question is in part supplied by the

Apostle Paul who throughout his epistles employs the Greek word *parakalein* (to exhort, to counsel, to comfort, etc) as his way of acting like a "human paraclete"—a minister—for his children in the faith. Thus, he counseled the Thessalonian Christians (1Thess 4:1) who had been witnessing the dying of fellow Christians to remember that they should not grieve as other people who have no hope beyond the grave (4:13).[7] So, Christians may indeed mourn as other human beings do. Such is the nature of mortality. Nevertheless, in Jesus Christ, they have a hope which is based on the resurrection of their Lord and his anticipated *parousia* (coming presence/return) in order to receive his followers into glory with him (4:14-17).

That marvelous hope, Paul announces, should comfort and console (*parakeite*) the Christians who had lost loved ones (4:18). Such a sense of hope in the midst of grief will certainly be used by the Holy Spirit today in touching others with the good news of Jesus Christ. Even in the traumatic experiences of our mourning, God can touch others with divine grace. Do not ever think that God is helpless because God is able to use us even in our weaknesses to confront others with the good news of the divine work in the world.

Needing direction. John includes a summary statement of the Holy Spirit's role in the life of the believer. In the midst of the disciples mourning over the immanent "departure" of Jesus, the caring Lord added that although they were filled with sorrow and could hardly bear to hear more (16:12), he had for them a concluding insight concerning the role of the Holy Spirit which is of crucial importance. Walking through life is a hazardous task, but the Christian has the resource of the Holy Spirit to be the guide for life (16:13). Anyone who has camped in a desert or wilderness like the Sinai knows the importance of having a guide to lead you because the way can be very confusing and you can easily become lost. Similarly, no matter what comes one's way in life, it is imperative for the Christian to realize that God has supplied a divine guide to lead the believer through the wildernesses of life. Even though one may not see the way ahead as one stares through one's tears, the Lord knows the way and the Spirit will not leave or abandon the Christian.

The Spirit will guide and direct your path and the paths of those you love. This promise is the foundation for authentic Christian ministering to those who face death and grief.

Conclusion

This task of ministering to those who are grieving is an onerous one that demands the ability to reach beyond the resources of human wisdom and understanding. It requires a living sense of God's presence in the life of a Christian. And it relies upon a vital understanding of God's power and the actual anticipation of the return of Christ Jesus to receive all who follow him. It does not focus on rules or mere words of confession to guarantee a living sense of destiny with God. Instead, it is based or founded on a life which is rooted in a living relationship with the eternal God who has indelibly touched the world in the incarnate Christ Jesus who personally lived among humans, experienced the reality of temptation, knew the pangs of hunger and thirst, felt the stings of rejection, then suffered, died and rose again from a real death in order that he might bring to the world a new and living hope.

When, at the end of chapter 20, John in his gospel wrote that "Jesus did many other signs which are not written in this book," he was merely detailing the fact that even his gospel could only cover a small selection of the acts of Jesus. But John was quick to add that what had been included in his gospel was clearly penned in order that the reader "might believe" that Jesus is truly the world's "messianic leader" and none other than the "Son of God" so that believing in him would indeed supply life, hope and an eternal destiny for all his followers (cf. John 20:30-31).

Therefore, to those who are weighed down by pain and suffering, as well as the reality of death and grieving, this Jesus offers to lift the veil of what might seem to be an otherwise clouded future (cf. Rev 1:1-3) so as to give insight, hope and power in facing the difficulties of life on earth. Whatever ministry God may have given to any of us, we should be assured that through the Holy Spirit, God has also provided the means and strength to accomplish that work.

Therefore, to the Triune God be all glory forever and ever. Amen.

Notes

[1]For my further comments on these verses see Gerald L. Borchert, "The Resurrection: 1 Corinthians 15" in *Review and Expositor*, 80.3 (Summer 1983), 401-415.

[2]See my comments in Gerald Borchert, "Revelation" in the *NLT Study Bible* (Carol Stream, IL: Tyndale House Publishers, 2008), 2196.

[3]For a detailed analysis of the Lazarus story in John's gospel please see my comments in Gerald L. Borchert, *John 1-11* in Vol. 25A, The New American Commentary (Nashville: Broadman and Holman, 1996), 348-363.

[4]For a detailed analysis of this section in John's gospel please see my comments in Gerald L. Borchert, *John 12-21* in Vol. 25B, The New American Commentary (Nashville: Broadman and Holman, 2002), 101-184.

[5]As I indicated in my commentary (*Ibid*, 121, n.141) contemporary teachings in Islam completely twist the meaning of this text and suggest that Mohammed fulfills the coming of another Paraclete.

[6]As I indicated in my commentary (*Ibid*, 124-25) the folk-tradition that is sometimes suggested by some well-meaning Pentecostals that the Spirit is "with" Christians but is "in" those who have received the so-called second blessing lacks an adequate basis for interpreting this gospel.

[7]For a further analysis of this section of 1Thessalonians please see my comments in Gerald L Borchert, *Discovering Thessalonians* in The Guideposts Home Bible Study Programs (Carmel, NY: Guideposts, 1986), 65-73.

It's Hard to Say Goodbye: Grief from a Pastoral Care Perspective

William L. Blevins, Ph. D., LMFT, LPC
Professor of Counseling, School of Nursing and Behavioral Health and School of Religion
Carson-Newman College

For everything there is a season, and a time for
every matter under heaven;
a time to be born, and a time to die;
a time to weep, and a time to laugh;
a time to mourn, and a time to dance;
a time to embrace, and
a time to refrain from embracing
(Eccl 3:1-5).

CAROL WAS A VERY CONSCIENTIOUS STUDENT. That reason is why I was curious about her absence from class. And that reason is why, a few days later, I stopped her in the hallway outside my office. Our conversation was brief and went something like the following:

"Hi, Carol. I missed you in class last week."

"Thanks. My grandfather died and I attended his funeral."

"I'm very sorry to hear that. Was his death unexpected?"

"Not really. His health had been declining for sometime. We knew he didn't have long to live.
But it was still a shock . . . you know, it's just hard to say goodbye."

"It is hard to say goodbye!" I knew immediately what Carol meant. For at that time my father was slowly dying of cancer. He had been suffering with this disease for over three years. During that time, we talked on several occasions about his impending death. Such talk was difficult for both of us. Yet the process of saying goodbye as he died was just as natural as saying hello when I was born.

Our effort to say goodbye was not always vocal. I recall one particular day when he was in the hospital. The previous night had been very restless for him. He had not slept. He had not been lucid. But he had agonized again with the intense pain from the tumor residing in his body. Now, hours later and heavily sedated, he appeared to be comatose. IV's penetrated his arms. Oxygen was being pumped into his lungs. He lay very still.

I had been sitting beside my Dad for a long while. My hand rested on his bed. Staring at an empty chair, I was lost in my own thoughts—reflecting on how much I loved him, how much I would miss him, and how I hurt for him. At that moment I felt him move. He slowly reached out to grasp my hand. He squeezed my hand hard. Then I looked at him. His eyes were closed, but tears lined his face. Tears lined my face too. And for a long while we simply held hands. There were no words. There was only silence. Yet instinctively I knew what was happening. We were both struggling to say goodbye.

The Nature of Grief

The word "grief" is a label we use for an experience that is universal and common to all persons who inhabit this planet. That label, however, is simply a label which points beyond itself to an array of complex human emotions and behaviors. For this reason, we must differentiate the words used to describe the experience from the experience itself. The two ideas are not identical. Grief is not an assortment of words contained in a dictionary. It is an emotional event that is processed deep within the human spirit and psyche. That event cannot be expressed fully with words. In fact, there are some aspects of this event that are completely inarticulate. They are mere "groanings which cannot be uttered" (Rom 8:26).

Although words cannot exhaust the complexity of the grief experience, they do enable us to understand and manage the experience. The words themselves become important because they literally shape how we think about grief and they influence how we experience grief. In part, this phenomenon happens because thoughts shape the brain chemistry that controls our moods and behavior.[1] Simply put, how we think about grief partially helps us to process and grow through grief.

Grief is an emotional and physiological response to any significant loss.

Usually, grief is most intense with the loss of a loved one, but it is not limited to death. Grief occurs with the loss of a spouse in divorce, a miscarriage, moving away from home, the loss of property or possessions, the loss of a job, the loss of health, the termination of a friendship, the loss of mobility, the loss of financial stability, or the loss of any other object for which one has developed a deep attachment. The loss can be real or imagined, temporary or permanent, avoidable or unavoidable, anticipated or unexpected. Yet, whatever its complexion, the grief experience always results from a significant loss, a loss that "crushes the spirit" (Prov 15:13). Grief is especially present in the death of a loved one.

Grief is holistic.

We are holistic (whole) beings, possessing several dimensions—which are physical, emotional, cognitive, social, and spiritual. Jesus referred to this nature of personhood when he described the healing of a man on the Sabbath: " . . . I made an entire [ὅλον] man well [ὑγιῆ] . . ." (John 7:23). The Greek word translated "entire" in this text is transliterated into English as "holon" from which the word holistic derives. Both words (holon and holistic) are used frequently in healthcare and mental health circles to describe the wholeness of a person. Our holistic nature means that all of the various dimensions of personhood (physical, emotional, cognitive, social, and spiritual) are inseparably related to each other. What affects one area affects all areas in some manner. To describe grief as being holistic means that it impacts one's total being. Not one dimension of our personhood is unaffected by the turbulent emotional undercurrents generated by painful loss. Grief is a holistic event.

Grief manifests itself with numerous symptoms.

The following symptoms are directly related to our holistic nature.

There are **physical s**ymptoms, such as shock, numbness, loss of appetite, difficulty sleeping, crying, assorted aches and pains (especially in the cardiovascular region), shortness of breath, difficulty swallowing, lack of energy, and the worsening of chronic health conditions.

There are **emotional** signs, such as depression, sadness, hopeless feelings, anxiety, anger, guilt, forgetfulness, resentment, fear, loneliness and the like.

There are **cognitive** symptoms such as the inability to concentrate, catastrophic thoughts, confusion, nightmares, negative thoughts, and even auditory or visual hallucinations.

There are **social** symptoms like increased frustration with others, a tendency to isolate oneself from others, an increased reliance upon others, impatience with others, and a diminished capacity to care for others.

And, of course, there are **spiritual** symptoms such as a loss of meaning in daily activities, apathy towards life in general, questioning why God permitted the loss, a sometimes reduced interest in religious services, a sense of disconnection with one's spiritual roots, or anger towards God. There are numerous symptoms and they vary in length and intensity.

The ones mentioned here are common examples, but the list is not complete. The point is that grief affects the whole person in diverse ways. The symptoms vary according to the nature of the loss, the health of the mourner, the quality of one's support group, how long one has been grieving, and countless existential factors in one's life. While the feelings and other symptoms can be extremely distressing and overwhelming, they are most often normal reactions to the pain accompanying the loss.

Grief is a complex reaction that is seldom static from one day to the next.

Grief is not one experience that maintains the same intensity, emotional reactions, or behavioral expressions from day to day or month to month. Grief is a process that is continually changing from onset to resolution (although in some situations there may not be a complete and final resolution). For this reason, most researchers describe grief as a process that has several stages.

Viewing grief as having stages can be helpful for both individual coping and professional treatment, but researchers differ about the number and character of the stages. Some identify as few as three or four stages while others recognize as many as ten. While there is no universal agreement, or clinical evidence to validate grief having stages, there is a consensus that grief is not the same for everyone.[2] In personal experience, the supposed stages do not always follow the same pattern, nor do they contain the same emotional quality. Sometimes the stages happen simultaneously and some of the stages do not happen at all. What is obvious is that persons tend to grieve in their own individual manner. In this regard, the grief process is more like a wave that is full of ups and downs, highs and lows, a wave that persistently comes and goes with fluctuating intensity. The entire process varies over time. Both the strength of emotions and the duration of the process are driven by factors common to the person who is mourning.

Grief does not run on a timely schedule and it is not regulated by a clock.

There is no normal timetable for grieving that works for everyone. Following the initial shock and numbness that often accompanies the onset of grief, some persons begin coping better after months of struggling with emotional distress. Others measure their progress in years. It is also not uncommon for a person to reach a certain level of healing (adjustment) in the grief process and then regress to an earlier phase. Or, some might "get stuck" (fixated) at a certain phase in the process and not progress for an indefinite period. If this particular situation becomes chronic, along with signals such as denial, continued social withdrawal, and a pronounced inability to cope on a daily basis, the individual might need professional help to get "unstuck."

The point here is that there are numerous variables that determine the length and intensity of grieving, including the nature of the loss, one's coping ability, the quality of the relationship with the deceased, the emotional health of the mourner, and the onset of grief. For instance, the grief process does not begin when the loss actually occurs. A person usually begins grieving when he or she first learns about the possibility of a loved one's death. My father was given a life expectancy of eighteen months along with his cancer diagnosis and I began grieving the day he received the diagnosis. This particular situation is called anticipatory grief. Because of the timeless nature of the grief experience, it is important to be patient with others and ourselves, allowing the process to develop naturally. Healing, like grief, is a process, but one must grieve in his or her own way and in his or her own time.

Grief is a gift.

Grief is neither comfortable nor trivial. It takes time. It is painful. It impacts the quality of life. It scars the soul. It shapes daily existence. It influences physical and emotional health. It consumes one's energy. One can safely conclude that grief is not a pleasant experience. Understanding such facts, however, is not a recent discovery. The difference between the pain of grief and the joy of happiness was recognized long ago: "A glad heart makes a happy face; a broken heart crushes the spirit" (Prov 15:13). Yet, although grief is not basically a pleasant event, it is indeed a divine gift.

One of the characteristics of the world which God has made is that everything in human experience changes. Everything from molecules to mountains are continuously in a state of flux. There is indeed a certain rhythm to life, a time to be born and a time to die, as well as a time to mourn and a time to dance. Life changes, things come to an end, including human life. How do we cope with this vulnerability? God has gifted us with the capacity to grieve. One does not have to take medicine to grieve. One does not have to be taught how to grieve. We humans do so naturally. God has built it into our emotional system. The ability to grieve is not pleasant, but it is natural and normal. Grief enables us to heal the past so we can go forward with our future. It empowers us to cope with tremendous losses and adjust in an appropriate manner to a world wherein everything changes and ends. The ability to grieve is God's gift that enables us to endure fragile life situations.

Helping Others Grieve

Jesus once pronounced a blessing upon those who mourn: "Blessed are those who mourn, for they shall be comforted"(Matt 5:4). Although his words appear to refer to one who experiences grief, the meaning may also include the opposite. In this particular instance, the "mourner" may be the one who cares for those who are suffering, such as Jesus lamenting over residents in Jerusalem (Luke 13:34). Consider the context of Jesus' statement. He often encountered persons who were emotionally exhausted and burdened. They were persons who needed "rest" (Matt 11:28-29). Regularly, he offered hope to persons who were barely surviving in an unjust and violent society. Life was cheap and people were trapped in a hopeless, pathetic existence, that was punctuated by apathy and indifference (Luke 13:34). His world was one where God's rule was mostly ignored. That reason is why he taught his disciples to pray that God's will would "be done on earth as it is in heaven"(Matt 6:10). In this context, a "mourner" refers to one who mourns over a world wherein God's will (justice and righteousness) is in eclipse. A mourner includes one who observes the sufferings of others, cares about their condition, and labors to rectify their situation according to God's will. The mourner focuses upon the aberrant plight of society in general and of persons who are hurting in particular.

As followers of Jesus today, do we not have a duty to minister to those who are grieving, who have experienced loss? Does Jesus not actually want us to care for others? Do we not have a responsibility to reach out to those who hurt? Does it not matter that God's will is often absent in societal, cultural, political, and corporate affairs? Does it not include religious matters as well? Do we not cry (mourn) over persons who are suffering? Of course, these questions are rhetorical and the answers are obvious. We have a divine calling to comfort those who suffer (2 Cor 1:3). How then do we translate this calling into practical, everyday behaviors that communicate care, understanding, and support for those who are grieving? Creating a "ministry of comfort" for the bereaved does not require a degree in mental health, but it does involve several practical skills.

Effective ministering of comfort requires a genuine caring and empathic spirit.

This characteristic is not the result of genetic influence. It is not a trait one brings from the womb. An empathic attitude, however, can be nurtured and it is one aspect of spiritual growth. Helen Keller, who never experienced sight, had impeccable insight into the human condition. She eloquently expressed that our life is not in vain when we care about another's pain:

> *We bereaved are not alone. We belong to the largest company in all the world, the company of those who have known suffering. When it seems that our sorrow is too great to be borne, let us think of the great family of the heavy hearted into which our grief has given us entrance, and inevitably, we will feel about us their arms, their sympathy, their understanding.*

> *Believe, when you are most unhappy, that there is something for you to do in the world. So long as you can sweeten another's pain, life is not in vain.*[3]

For a group of dispirited and dejected disciples, Jesus referred to the Holy Spirit as "the Comforter" (John 14:16, 26; 15:26; 16:7). Paul used a form of the same Greek word (*parakalein*) to describe God's response to our suffering, as well as our responsibility to comfort others who are hurting (2 Cor 1:3-4). To use Henri Nouwen's phrase, we are all "wounded healers" who recognize that grief is one of life's most painful events.[4] In order to minister effectively to others who are grieving, we must first cultivate an attitude of compassion, warmth, kindness, and empathy in ourselves. The ability to comfort others requires a genuinely caring spirit.

Helping others means encouraging them to talk about what they are experiencing.

Some years ago, a physician made an appointment to talk with me about his wife's death from breast cancer, which occurred four months earlier. He and his wife had been married for twenty years and had three sons. For most of the hour, the doctor agonized over her death, freely venting his emotions and sharing the agonizing struggle to recreate a world without his wife. "It is so difficult," he said, "to make **our** bedroom **my** bedroom, and **our** closet **my** closet, and **our** bathroom **my** bathroom." With these words, he punctuated the powerful emotions of loss that reverberated deep inside his spirit and were challenging the strenuous uncompleted work of his adjustment.

Whenever persons express their grief in an emotionally safe environment, several positive results can facilitate the grief process. Each time persons recount their story they gain new insight into what they are experiencing. This retelling facilitates emotional healing. In addition, current research in the area of neuroscience suggests that grappling with issues such as this one can enhance healthy brain functioning, as well as facilitate spiritual growth.[5] Both enable grieving in a healthy manner.

Becoming an effective comforter involves attentive, supportive listening.

Listening without judging or giving unwanted advice is in itself an encouragement for persons to share their pain, and it provides an opportunity for them to re-grieve, which also enables healing. The goal of attentive listening is not to "cheer up" the mourner or make the person "feel better." The objective of supportive listening is to hear, understand, empathize, and support the mourner. Whenever we invalidate, minimize, or discount another's feelings, beliefs, or experiences we cease to comforters. Remember Job's reaction to his alleged friends. As he struggled to make it through each day, his friends offered empty words rather than a supportive presence. Frustrated, hurting, and feeling abandoned, Job lamented: "I have heard many things like these; miserable comforters are you all!"(Job 16:2). Job's friends offered platitudes, but not themselves. A helpful comforter displays a supportive and attentive attitude.

Simply being present is one of the most effective ways to be a comforter.

To be present means being available in a caring, supportive, and understanding manner. Remember Jesus' experience in Gethsemane the night of his arrest! Jesus was "sorrowful and deeply troubled" and like most persons experiencing acute grief, he wanted his disciples to be with him in those moments (Matt 26:37). On several occasions that night, he begged his disciples to watch with him, but they merely slept (26:38-44). Coping with deep emotions is always affected by the quality of one's support group. The presence of a faithful and caring support group, even if the group is only one person, enables the mourner to bear the pain of grief more effectively. Whenever the support group is absent or inadequate, the experience for the mourner is more difficult.[6] Effective comforters provide an affirming presence.

Managing Our Own Grief

As mentioned above, Henri Nouwen referred to Christians as "wounded healers." Both words are significant for those of us who bear the name of Jesus. We are "healers" in the sense that we minister to others in a caring and compassionate manner that facilitates their healing. We are also "wounded" because we are not immune to the inevitable sufferings of this world. So far as grief is concerned, we must all experience the depths of emotional distress and agonizing pain that accompanies loss. This fact means that we must learn how to manage our own grief adequately. How then do we cope with our own wounds?

There are many ways that we can cope with our own struggles with loss. Managing grief in a healthy manner involves practical behaviors such as being open about death, participating in religious services, eventually establishing closure with the deceased, continually recognizing and processing our emotions, and maintaining our spirituality in whatever ways we find meaningful. These processes are only a few of the ways we manage grief appropriately. There are, however, two especially essential responses that enable us to cope effectively with grief—openness to others and faith in God.

Managing grief is enabled by openness to those who care.

We are told that Jesus regularly traveled through the towns and villages of Galilee, preaching the good news of the kingdom (Luke 8:1). The twelve disciples accompanied him, along with several prominent women who "ministered" to him from their resources (Luke 8:2-3). The word translated "ministered" (*diakanoun*) is a verbal form of our English word "deacon." Literally, these women "deaconed" him. There is also another reference about angels ministering to Jesus after his temptation experience in the wilderness (Mark 1:13). The same verb is used there. The angels "deaconed" him. The point here is that even Jesus sometimes needed and received encouragement from others. If it was true for Jesus, how much more is it true for us? You and I are not above our Lord. We all need support from others. Although we are called to be ministers of comfort **to** others, we also need the ministry of comfort **from** others. Our ability to handle grief depends, in part, upon our openness to accepting this gift.

The strength that comes from others became especially real for me beginning on August 28, 2004. On that day, the day of my mother's funeral, we discovered that our youngest daughter had been murdered. I cannot begin to describe the emotional implosion which was triggered by the words "Dad, Kym is dead!" It was a terse message from my son who discovered her body. And I do not have words to describe how I felt when I repeated those very words to my wife before we collapsed into each other's arms, holding each other as though our world seemed to be falling apart, which it was. As never before, I realized that not one of us is truly adequate in ourselves for life. We need each other. Over the next few months we received many gifts from friends and neighbors, everything from baked goods to flowers, from emails to candles. We were appreciative and grateful for the generous and caring responses from so many persons. But what encouraged us the most was simply the fact that people were there for us and with us. They supported us when we struggled, and hugged us when we cried. These friends "deaconed" us and that was most empowering.

Managing grief involves using our faith.

As followers of Jesus, we not only **have** faith, **we live by** faith. The affirmation, "the just shall live by faith," is mentioned three times in the New Testament (Rom 1:17; Gal 3:11; Heb 10:38), and with the exception of a small particle in one reference all three statements are exactly the same (*ho de dikaios ek pisteos* *zesetai*). Faith is not optional for those desiring to follow Jesus. It is synonymous with following Jesus. Although it is translated "believe," the Greek text declares that whoever "continues faithing" (believing) Jesus has eternal life (John 3:16). With faith we begin our journey with Jesus, and with faith we cope with life's obstacles (Matt 17:20). Surviving loss is no exception. In managing our own grief, faith becomes **a therapeutic tool**.

Consider these questions: How often does Scripture proclaim that God is there for us, in all circumstances, actively working for our good (Rom 8:28)? How many instances does the Bible speak of a merciful God who "comforts us in our affliction" (2 Cor 1:3-4)? How often does Scripture refer to God's abiding love and care for us? We are assured of his presence, no matter what our life situation might be:

> *I am convinced that there is nothing in death or life, in the realm of spirits or superhuman powers, in the world as it is or the world as it shall be, in the forces of the universe, in heights or depths—nothing in all creation can separate us from the love of God in Christ Jesus our Lord.* (Rom 8:31-39)

The Bible affirms that the just shall **live** by faith. We should not overlook the importance of the word "live." Living is what we do each day. It involves trivial issues like shopping at the market or filling the car with gas. It involves meaningful activities like sharing an outing with family, attending a daughter's recital, or bringing flowers on an anniversary. It involves mandatory behaviors like completing tasks at work or school. And sometimes living involves wrestling with turbulent undercurrents of emotions sparked by the loss of a loved one. In those moments of loss—the cold, frightful, devastating terrible moments—we are not alone, nor are we destroyed. God is there for us: "He heals the brokenhearted and binds up their wounds" (Ps 147:3). Through faith in him we can endure all things (Phil 4:13).

Conclusion

So, how did I survive my daughter's death, one of the most profound defining moments of my life? I have been asked that question countless times since that August morning in 2004. How was I able to process those awe-full emotions and maintain my sanity? How do I now make it through each day with the memories? How will I find the strength I will need for tomorrow? My answer has been, and will always be, the same—through faith and friends. I cope with loss through the strength of faith and friends. Both are as empowering as they are therapeutic.

Notes

[1]Louis Cozolino, *The Neuroscience of Psychotherapy: Building and Rebuilding the Human Brain* (New York: W. W. Norton and Company, 2002), 94-98.

[2]Coval B. MacDonald, *"Loss and Bereavement,"* in *Clinical Handbook of Pastoral Counseling*, edited by Robert J. Wicks, Richard D. Parsons, and Donald E. Capps (New York: Doubleday, 1972), 539-543.

[3]Helen Keller, *We Bereaved* (New York: Fuldenwider, 1929).

[4]Henri J. M. Nouwen, *The Wounded Healer: Ministry in Contemporary Society* (New York: Doubleday, 1972), xv-xvi.

[5]Andrew Newberg, MD, and Mark Robert Waldman, *How God Changes Your Brain: Breakthrough Findings from a Leading Neuroscientist* (New York: Ballantine Books, 2010), 162-163.

[6]Dean Ornish, MD, *Love and Survival* (New York; Harper Collins, 1999), 199-125.

How Jesus Interpreted Tragedy[1]

Donald W. Garner, Ph. D.
Professor, School of Religion
Carson-Newman College

Disaster and Disorientation

A POWERFUL HURRICANE ROARS IN FROM the stormy ocean, slamming into the Carolina coast with destructive winds and flooding rains. After a few furious hours, the storm leaves catastrophic damage for hundreds of miles in its wake.

With little warning, a fierce tornado swoops down from the angry Kansas skies. The terrible twister explodes neighborhood homes into splinters and tumbles family cars like brutally crushed toys.

Wildfires in California are sparked by lightning and then fanned by the Santa Anna winds. The flames consume beautiful forests like match sticks, gobble up beloved homes like kindling, and swallow precious schools like cardboard boxes.

Following any such natural disaster, its victims often wail: "Why did God do this to me?" Then, when our legal system cannot assign any human liability for these mammoth losses, insurance adjusters will label the entire calamity as "an act of God."

It is no wonder that so many of us—even many Christians—become confused and even shattered when tragedy strikes us. Not only are we reeling from the disorientation of personal loss and grief. But, from the biblical perspective, we are suffering from "a double disorientation" because we also have been misinformed by a seriously misleading theological error!

Jesus Tried to Correct Our Erroneous Ideas

Jesus clearly repudiated this very simplistic notion which so many of us carry around in our confused minds and broken hearts. He flatly rejected the widely popular notion that God brought these disasters upon us. He denied the hasty conclusion that one's suffering is **always** deserved because God is punishing our guilt resulting from some past wrong-doing.

In the Gospel record, we read about two different occasions when Jesus sought to straighten out a crooked theology that was widely popular but nevertheless quite hurtful. Just because it was a widespread teaching based upon a long-held tradition did not mean that it was correct. And Jesus certainly saw the wrong and the hurt it was causing. Two Gospel writers, John and Luke, both wanted us to understand how clearly Jesus tried to correct this seriously mistaken theology about human experiences of tragedy and catastrophe.

A family tragedy (John 9:1-5)

> [1] *As Jesus was walking along, he saw a man who had been blind from birth.* [2] *"Rabbi," his disciples asked him, "why was this man born blind? Was it because of his own sins or his parents' sins?"* [3] *"It was not because of his sins or his parents' sins," Jesus answered. "This happened so the power of God could be seen in him.* [4] *We must quickly carry out the tasks assigned us by the one who sent us. The night is coming, and then no one can work.* [5] *But while I am here in the world, I am the light of the world" (NLT).*

Excited about their pregnancy, and eagerly anticipating the arrival of their brand new baby, the faithful Jewish couple welcomed a newborn son into the world. But very soon after his birth, the baby gave evidence to his parents that something was different. It was his eyes. He did not focus his gaze upon their smiling faces. He did not blink when they snapped their fingers close to his eyes. Soon the painful truth became clear to them: he was not able to see with his eyes. He was born blind.

Science had not yet invented the Erythromycin ointment that now can sanitize the eyes of every newborn as soon as he or she passes through the birth canal and into the world. Infections which can rob a baby of eyesight are rare today in locations where good medical care is available. But in the time of Jesus, congenital blindness was much more common because health issues in newborns were left to chance—and then interpreted as an act of God.

So when they encountered the man born blind, the disciples asked Jesus to make known his position on such a case. They fully expected that Jesus would confirm a very typical Jewish conclusion: all tragedy is punishment for sin. "Teacher, who sinned in the past to result in this present tragedy?" A blind baby must prove that sin has happened somewhere. This sad situation was obvious evidence to us, Jesus, that somebody "messed up" and God punished them for their wrongdoing. Which member of this family caused this tragedy to happen? Who sinned? The father? The mother? Even the baby in the womb prior to his own birth? That is how far their mistaken theology was willing to go in order to support itself—even to blame the baby for some sinful behavior before his birth (after all, babies are active in the womb before birth, so maybe a part of that activity had been sinful).

But Jesus would have none of it! "Nobody sinned here to cause this problem. Period!"[2] His reply was simple and perfectly clear. That is the wrong approach to take in this deeply sad situation. Do not blame the victim—have not these people suffered enough without you loading false guilt on top of their burdensome weight of grief and loss? So instead of assigning blame and punishment here, let us look for God's presence and let us become a part of God's work of grace in this situation of pain.

When people are hurting, God is available—through the work of God's Son and his followers—to do the work of God's grace on their behalf. God's loving concern, unlike our theological curiosity, is not "Why?" but "What now?" Time is precious; and precious, too, is the work of God that brings light into the darkest situations which people can face. The "blame game" is easy for us to do, but all too often it is ill-placed, unkind, and just plain wrong. The "grace game" is what God has put us here to do. We are here to touch people's lives of painful brokenness with God's loving presence, gentle power, and renewed hope—which is the very Light of God in their difficult darkness.[3]

Unnatural deaths—terrorism and natural disasters (Luke 13:1-5)

> [1] *About this time Jesus was informed that Pilate had murdered some people from Galilee as they were offering sacrifices at the Temple.* [2] *"Do you think those Galileans were worse sinners than all the other people from Galilee?" Jesus asked. "Is that why they suffered?* [3] *Not at all! And you will perish, too, unless you repent of your sins and turn to God.* [4] *And what about the eighteen people who died when the tower in Siloam fell on them? Were they the worst sinners in Jerusalem?* [5] *No, and I tell you again that unless you repent, you will perish, too" (NLT).*

Jesus was asked one day about the calamity that had stricken some faithful Jews who had traveled to Jerusalem from his northern home region of Galilee. A cadre of Roman soldiers—those bitterly despised occupiers of the beloved Jewish homeland—encroached upon the Temple precincts and committed an unthinkable atrocity by slaughtering those Galilean Jewish worshippers, "mingling their blood with their sacrifices." Brutally interrupted in the middle of a worship service at the Temple, those innocent Jews were butchered like animals. And, in a bitter irony, their own blood literally flowed together on the paving stones with the blood of their animal sacrifices which they had just dedicated and given to God.

Since he was a rabbi and a skillful interpreter of the things of God, Jesus was presented with this extremely upsetting episode. And the questioners were ready to pose some very pointed religious problems for Jesus to solve. Why did God do such a thing to these good Jews? Why did such a horribly sad thing happen to such obviously good people? How could God punish these God-fearing Jews at the hands of such godless Romans? Where was the justice of God when these people encountered a tragic death they did not deserve?

Jesus anticipated where the discussion was going. So he said "out loud" what everyone around him was assuming in their heads and hearts. "Are you assuming that those people from Galilee died because they deserved it, because God was punishing them for their sins? Have you jumped to the conclusion that they were such bad sinners that God gathered them up and led them down to Jerusalem for worship so that God might justifiably wipe them out with the swords of the terrorizing Romans?" Of course, that is **exactly** what the listeners of Jesus were assuming!

But Jesus said flatly, "No." How many times in the pages of the Gospels does Jesus answer the questions posed to him with a clear "yes" or a flat "no?" Not very often—it is very, very rare. He usually answered a question with a question—or with a parable or a wise saying that sent people away scratching their heads concerning a Kingdom truth.

But, in this case, the issue was so important that he bluntly said: "Absolutely not. No way. You are wrong. Do not go there. And, by the way, let us talk about you, not them. So rather than speculate about **their** deaths as punishment for sin, you can be sure that if **you** are sinning then you will be punished."

And then Jesus immediately put forth another case study to drive home his teaching even more pointedly in the minds of his listeners. His example involved a natural disaster, not a case of human violence. A recent earthquake had shaken Jerusalem and brought down one of the towers that had been built into the city's outer defensive walls. When the stone structure collapsed, it fatally crushed eighteen unfortunate people beneath its rubble. No doubt, the event was big news when it happened. And Jesus drew out into the open some of the questions that always are lurking in people's minds after such a notorious catastrophe strikes.

"Do you think they deserved death, too—like those Temple worshippers from Galilee? Is that why they died—as God's punishment upon their sinful lives? Do you actually imagine that God was operating in the city of Jerusalem that day like an invisible sheepdog, herding together the very worst sinners in the city, bringing them to that one spot, and then popping them with the tower to kill them? Do you really believe that nonsense?!? I tell you absolutely not. But rather than speculate and assume that **their** deaths were due to sin, you should be reminded of the timeless biblical truth that **your** sin will lead to your death."

Notice that Jesus is reversing the order of their logic. He was saying to them, "You always assume that a death can be traced back to sin; but I tell you that the only real certainty is that sin will lead to death."

The order makes a significant difference in separating error from truth. And the proper order—as well as the mistaken reversal of the order—can be traced all the way back into the Old Testament. For centuries the Jews in large numbers, including the three friends of Job, had been misinterpreting God's revealed truth about sin and its consequences. And Jesus emphatically tried to correct their persistently wrong reading of Scripture.

Where Did Our Serious Error Begin?

Why did Jesus have to deal with this "backwards" notion of God's presence and role in human suffering? How did so many Jews of that day get the order reversed? How does the Bible draw the proper connection between sin and its negative consequences? And what was Jesus saying to them as he tried to help them to straighten out a common error?

Deuteronomy 28 has been labeled "the blessings and the curses" chapter. In this chapter we read so clearly stated an oft-repeated biblical truth that God will bless the righteous and punish the wicked. As Moses delivered his farewell address to the children of Israel, he reminded them of the commitment they made to God at Mt. Sinai. They had agreed to enter into a covenant relationship with God—He would be their God, and they would be his people.

And to follow God in faithfulness and obedience will result in blessing; but to turn away from God in rebellion and disobedience results in curses. If you obey, then you will be blessed . . . rewarded . . . life will go well; but if you disobey, then you will be cursed . . . punished . . . life will go poorly. Moses made the contrast quite clear.

> [1] *"If you fully obey the LORD your God and carefully keep all his commands that I am giving you today, the LORD your God will set you high above all the nations of the world.* [2] *You will experience all these blessings if you obey the LORD your God:*
> [3] *Your towns and your fields will be blessed.* [4] *Your children and your crops will be blessed. The offspring of your herds and flocks will be blessed.* [5] *Your fruit baskets and breadboards will be blessed.* [6] *Wherever you go and whatever you do, you will be blessed.*
> [7] *"The LORD will conquer your enemies when they attack you. They will attack you from one direction, but they will scatter from you in seven!*
> [8] *"The LORD will guarantee a blessing on everything you do and will fill your storehouses with grain. The*

LORD your God will bless you in the land he is giving you.

[9] *"If you obey the commands of the LORD your God and walk in his ways, the LORD will establish you as his holy people as he swore he would do.* [10] *Then all the nations of the world will see that you are a people claimed by the LORD, and they will stand in awe of you.*

[11] *"The LORD will give you prosperity in the land he swore to your ancestors to give you, blessing you with many children, numerous livestock, and abundant crops.* [12] *The LORD will send rain at the proper time from his rich treasury in the heavens and will bless all the work you do. You will lend to many nations, but you will never need to borrow from them.* [13] *If you listen to these commands of the LORD your God that I am giving you today, and if you carefully obey them, the LORD will make you the head and not the tail, and you will always be on top and never at the bottom.* [14] *You must not turn away from any of the commands I am giving you today, nor follow after other gods and worship them.*

[15] *"But if you refuse to listen to the LORD your God and do not obey all the commands and decrees I am giving you today, all these curses will come and overwhelm you:*

[16] Your towns and your fields will be cursed. [17] Your fruit baskets and breadboards will be cursed. [18] Your children and your crops will be cursed. The offspring of your herds and flocks will be cursed. [19] Wherever you go and whatever you do, you will be cursed.

[20] "The LORD himself will send on you curses, confusion, and frustration in everything you do, until at last you are completely destroyed for doing evil and abandoning me. [21] The LORD will afflict you with diseases until none of you are left in the land you are about to enter and occupy. [22] The LORD will strike you with wasting diseases, fever, and inflammation, with scorching heat and drought, and with blight and mildew. These disasters will pursue you until you die. [23] The skies above will be as unyielding as bronze, and the earth beneath will be as hard as iron. [24] The LORD will change the rain that falls on your land into powder, and dust will pour down from the sky until you are destroyed.

[25] "The LORD will cause you to be defeated by your enemies. You will attack your enemies from one direction, but you will scatter from them in seven! You will be an object of horror to all the kingdoms of the earth. [26] Your corpses will be food for all the scavenging birds and wild animals, and no one will be there to chase them away. (Deut 28:1-26, *NLT*)

"The Deuteronomic Theology of History" says that God will reward the righteous and punish the wicked. That is the theological theme that binds together as one story the many episodes that are retold throughout the books of Deuteronomy, Joshua, Judges, 1-2 Samuel, and 1-2 Kings—a collection which constitutes "The Deuteronomic History" of ancient Israel's story in scripture.

Maintain the Sinai Covenant faithfully and God will be faithful to you with the outflow of God's blessings. Disobey the Mosaic Law and repudiate your relationship of faithfulness to God, and you can expect to be held accountable by God and to pay a price of lost blessings. Remember that the Old Testament prophets took this very same theology and preached it—before, during, and after the Babylonian Exile (with all of its own tragedies and horrors). The simple truth is that "sin results in punishment."

Of course, the challenge of Deuteronomy 28 is absolutely true; but the **reversal** of its truth is too often very false. Yes, it is true, all sin results in "cursing"—punishment, bad things, judgment, suffering, loss. Not all suffering and loss, however, is the direct result of sin in the one who is suffering. There is such a thing as innocent suffering that is neither deserved nor fair.

Yet, back in Old Testament times, God's people "turned it all around"—they frequently had it **backwards**. And Jesus knew it. He saw their error. And he **said** it was erroneous. Yet we keep repeating it today because we have not heard and received as God's grace the powerful truth that Jesus taught about tragedy.

A classic example of the error—Job's friends

The three friends of Job meant well. They came to help him in his suffering. And their first response to his painfully tragic losses was deep sensitivity and careful thoughtfulness (Job 2:11-13). But the raw honesty of Job's pain (Job 3:1ff) soon frightened them.

They always had known their good friend to be a righteous man of deep integrity, yet they now saw his intense suffering. How could they explain such multiple catastrophes in his life, one after the other? How could they help him find his way out of such deep hurt? Could they help bring some order back to his life of utter disorientation?

They reached the conclusion together that anyone who was "cursed" to this extent **must** have committed sin to bring about such suffering. They assumed that his current suffering was directly traceable to his previous sin. They committed the serious mistake of reversing the truth and turning it around backwards. They jumped from "sin-produces-curses/punishment /suffering" to "suffering proves sin."

We can give a name or label to this mistake in their logic—I call it "the mirror error." A mirror reverses our appearance. My hair is not really parted on the left—but it certainly looks that way in the mirror. When I am looking at myself in the mirror, the flip-flop reversal of my head and hairdo is not a serious matter if I am merely brushing my hair on any normal morning. But if things get really serious, as when I begin to cut my hair with scissors, then the mirror error can cause a serious blood-letting! I am likely to cut my ear if I try to cut my hair by looking in the mirror. So I pay Cathy good money to cut my hair every few weeks (because she does not have to look in the mirror to do the job)! The mirror error fails me, if I cut it myself, just when things get really serious near my ears.

That description is a rough analogy for how serious the reversal of the biblical truth of "sin-produces-suffering" can be. Not all suffering is the result of sin. Jesus said it. The brutal death of Jesus proves it. There **are** innocent sufferers. Job was such a person—but his helpful friends could never see or admit it was true. So please do not commit the mirror error every time you see suffering/curses in someone's life and quickly assume that the hurting person deserved it and brought this calamity upon himself.

Seriously mistaken because they were so tightly wedded to the mirror error, the friends of Job proceeded to berate him with their "backwards" assumptions. Anyone could see that Job was suffering at a deep level. Such suffering, they concluded, could only be explained one way—he deserved it. He must have brought all of this calamity down upon himself. After all, does not sin produce suffering in God's world? Then suffering must mean there was sin, right?[4] Notice the mirror at work. It is subtle, but very serious in the reversal that results.

The flip-flop mistake which his friends made caused them to add significantly to Job's grief. He resisted their interpretation of his situation and told them that he did not deserve what had happened to him. And that stubbornness in Job's responses to their "mirror error" interpretations of his situation convinced them even more that he was trying to deny or cover up the sin they were sure he had done. Their "help" for him soon degenerated into a full-blown shouting match. It was not a pretty picture—and it was a long way from the friendly chats and deep sharing that the four of them once enjoyed together.

Eliphaz told Job that nobody would be punished like he was hurting unless he really was guilty of something:

> [3] *"In the past you have encouraged many people; you have strengthened those who were weak.* [4] *Your words have supported those who were falling; you encouraged those with shaky knees.*
> [5] *But now when trouble strikes, you lose heart. You are terrified when it touches you.*
> [6] *Doesn't your reverence for God give you confidence? Doesn't your life of integrity give you hope?*
> [7] *"Stop and think! Do the innocent die? When have the upright been destroyed?* [8] *My experience shows that those who plant trouble and cultivate evil will harvest the same.* [9] *A breath from God destroys them. They vanish in a blast of his anger.* (Job 4:3-9, *NLT*)

And Bildad encouraged Job to go ahead and confess all of his sinfulness to a just God so that God could forgive him and then everything would be okay again:

> [3]*Does God twist justice? Does the Almighty twist what is right?* [4]*Your children must have sinned against him, so their punishment was well deserved.* [5] *But if you pray to God and seek the favor of the Almighty,* [6]*and if you are pure and live with integrity, he will surely rise up and restore your happy home.* [7]*And though you started with little, you will end with much.* (Job 8:3-7, *NLT*)

Job's most zealous and obnoxious friend, Zophar, told Job that even though he had lost everything except his wife and his life (he had even lost his health), God had not punished Job nearly as much as he deserved:

> [2] *"Shouldn't someone answer this torrent of words? Is a person proved innocent just by a lot of talking?* [3]*Should I remain silent while you babble on? When you mock God, shouldn't someone make you ashamed?* [4]*You claim, 'My beliefs are pure,' and 'I am clean in the sight of God.'* [5]*If only God would speak; if only he would tell you what he thinks!* [6] *If only he would tell you the secrets of wisdom, for true wisdom is not a simple matter. Listen! God is doubtless punishing you far less than you deserve!*
>
> [13] *"If only you would prepare your heart and lift up your hands to him in prayer!* [14]*Get rid of your sins, and leave all iniquity behind you.*

> [15] *Then your face will brighten with innocence.*
> *You will be strong and free of fear.*
>
> [16]*You will forget your misery; it will be like water flowing away.* [17]*Your life will be brighter than the noonday. Even darkness will be as bright as morning.* [18]*Having hope will give you courage. You will be protected and will rest in safety.* [19]*You will lie down unafraid, and many will look to you for help.* [20]*But the wicked will be blinded. They will have no escape.* (Job 11:2-6, 13-20, *NLT*)

These three friends of Job genuinely thought that they were telling the truth of Deuteronomy 28. They really were sincere even while they were being so insensitive (note the fact that they were **not** the ones who were suffering). And, as a side benefit, they looked good in contrast to Job's plight—so they could feel quite smug about their own lives of righteousness and blessedness.

But, in fact, they blatantly had committed the "mirror error" because they had the truth turned around! They assumed that if one suffered or life went very poorly, then one must have been seriously disobedient. If one was blessed or life went well, then goodness certainly was receiving its just reward. Like an image in a mirror, their error looked and sounded very much like the truth. But it is not the truth, particularly in those subtle but serious cases where the truth really matters!

And, worst of all, they refused to listen to Job because he threatened their neat, self-serving religious system. They chose to attack their friend in order to preserve their theological conclusions and to protect their comfort zone of self-righteousness.

Jesus Corrects Our Backwards Thinking

The Book of Job was written to try to correct this ancient "mirror error" that was committed so obviously by the three friends. But Jesus was **still** dealing with the very same error in his day because his own disciples had not learned to avoid the "mirror error" of Job's friends. Their questions to Jesus revealed that they were thinking backwards about the truth and thus created a mistaken theology. "Who sinned, this man or his parents, that he was born blind?"

So Jesus gave a clear, emphatic "No!" to the false assumption that suffering always proves that sin is present. He returned to the correct order of Deuteronomy 28 when he said, "unless you repent of sin, then you will perish" (Luke 13:3,5). He replaced the mirror error with the straightforward truth: sin will produce suffering, but suffering does not necessarily prove sin.

And Jesus asserted that innocent suffering, the most tragic and perplexing kind, does in fact exist. Think of all of the innocent suffering that we can find recorded in scripture: Job, the Psalmist [49 of the psalms are laments], Jeremiah [read his Confessions], Herod's slaughter of the innocents, John the Baptist [imprisoned and beheaded], Paul's hardships for the sake of the gospel, and Jesus' own death as the ultimate statement of undeserved suffering and tragedy.

Jesus taught us, in his own terrible death, that obedience to God—and life with God, even in pain—is our choice. Jonah is our example of what not to do because he tried to run away from the negatives in his walk with God. Job is our positive example. He decided to try to take in stride all of the negatives he encountered on faith's highway. And Job steadfastly refused to let go of God in his life, even during his period of deep suffering. But he finally did not blame God or "an act of God"—he ultimately trusted God who came to him on the ash heap (Job 38-41).

Conclusion: Trusting Our Lives to God

In his closing paragraphs in the letter to the Galatians, Paul asserted precisely the same truth that was found in Deuteronomy 28, and in Jesus' clear teaching:

> [7] *Don't be misled—you cannot mock the justice of God. You will always harvest what you plant.* [8]*Those who live only to satisfy their own sinful nature will harvest decay and death from that sinful nature. But those who live to please the Spirit will harvest everlasting life from the Spirit.* [9]*So let's not get tired of doing what is good. At just the right time we will reap a harvest of blessing if we don't give up* (Gal 6:7-9, *NLT*).

We must **not** settle for a **mechanical system** of explanation that is backwards . . . a mirror error . . . that seems to work and that sounds fine to us most of the time—until we are the one who is suffering so intensely like Job did. And until that day when certain "friends" around us berate us with **their** need for us to be deserving of such a punishment!

We do find comfort in a **personal relationship** to God that never fails us, not in some mechanical explanation that itself is erroneous. We put our trust where Jesus himself placed his: in our faithfulness to God because we trust that God will be faithful to us.

> [5] *You must have the same attitude that Christ Jesus had.*
> [6] *Though he was God, he did not think of equality with God as something to cling to.* [7]*Instead, he gave up his divine privileges; he took the humble position of a slave and was born as a human being. When he appeared in human form,* [8]*he humbled himself in obedience to God and died a criminal's death on a cross.*
> [9]*Therefore, God elevated him to the place of highest honor and gave him the name above all other names,* [10]*that at the name of Jesus every knee should bow, in heaven and on earth and under the earth,* [11]*and every tongue confess that Jesus Christ is Lord, to the glory of God the Father.* (Phil 2:5-11, *NLT*)

We believe that if we are faithful to God—as Jesus was faithful through his suffering—then God will be faithful to us—as God was faithful to raise Jesus from the grave—no matter what comes into our lives.

Notes

[1]While the author was on an archaeological dig in Jordan, the oldest of his three sons was injured in a single-vehicle rollover accident in Durham, NC and spent eight days in the neurological intensive care unit at Duke Medical Center before brain death was determined on July 30, 1999. Aaron Garner was three weeks away from his junior year as a computer science major at Carson-Newman College when his body was buried in a family plot in Raleigh, NC. As Don was making his way home from the Middle East, he prayed and reflected and wrote most of the eulogy which he later read at the memorial service. Foremost in his prayerful struggle across those days were some of the biblical truths which he had taught to his students in the "Proverbs, Job, Ecclesiastes" course every spring for 20 years. Those concepts are the substance of this article, biblical truths from the study that have been confirmed in life's experience of deep pain and loss.

[2]While there are no punctuation marks in the Greek manuscripts it seems that a period captures the intention of Jesus in this verse. The effect is that Jesus actually said something like this: "No, neither this man nor his parents sinned at some time in the past. But now, since the situation is what it is, and so that the work of God might be done in their lives, let us engage this tragedy in a positive way. These poor people have been hurting in darkness long enough. Let's not waste any more time but help them now with God's work in their life. A theological

discussion **about** them should be replaced quickly with a work of grace **for** them."

[3]Remember the teaching of Jesus that his followers should treat even their enemies with grace because of the even-handed grace of God who gives rain and sunshine upon the crops of everyone — the just and the unjust.

> [43] *"You have heard the law that says, 'Love your neighbor' and hate your enemy.* [44] *But I say, love your enemies! Pray for those who persecute you!* [45] *In that way, you will be acting as true children of your Father in heaven. For he gives his sunlight to both the evil and the good, and he sends rain on the just and the unjust alike.* [46] *If you love only those who love you, what reward is there for that? Even corrupt tax collectors do that much.* [47] *If you are kind only to your friends, how are you different from anyone else? Even pagans do that.* [48] *But you are to be perfect, even as your Father in heaven is perfect* (Matt 5:43-48, *NLT*).

[4] And health and prosperity clearly mean that one is righteous and justifiably receiving the smiles of God, right? So, if suffering people (i.e., Job) are getting God's punishment for sin, then blessed people (i.e., the three friends) obviously are getting God's endorsement and "1st prize blue ribbon" of approval upon their lives. But, of course, our wealth may have come from greed, dishonesty, and theft—nothing which God could ever endorse! And our adversity may have come from forces beyond our control or responsibility. So the mirror error

serves both to hurt the sufferer and to allow the blessed one often to delude him or herself. In either case, it is to be avoided.

Where Is God When We Hurt?
A Pastoral Perspective

Harold T. Bryson, Th. D.
Senior Professor, School of Religion
Carson-Newman College

BOTH JESUS AND THE APOSTLES talked sparingly as they walked to Jerusalem on the way to the Feast of Passover. The Lord had much on his mind. He knew that "his hour had come" (John 13:1). As he walked, he must have reflected on his life and ministry with the apostles. He also must have anticipated the cruel response that he was going to receive from the religious leaders. He undoubtedly pondered the possibilities concerning his death. Natural human feelings must have come to Jesus–the rejection of those who should have known who he was, the false accusations that would be brought against him, the heartbreak of denials and betrayal by those close to him, and the dread of the inevitable suffering of crucifixion. "Jesus was troubled in spirit" (John 13:21). He had been exceptionally close to the apostles for some time and he was sad, knowing that he was going to leave them. Jesus, the unique Son of God, experienced what could be called "anticipatory grief" as he made his way to Jerusalem.

The apostles knew Jesus in a special way. They observed his actions and listened to his words. They also knew his non-verbal communication. They had the privilege of hearing many of his words. The trip to Jerusalem prompted questions from the apostles: Why was Jesus so quiet? What did Jesus have on his mind? Could the time be near when he assumed the role of a political Messiah and gained independence for the Jews from the Romans? The apostles knew that something weighed heavily on the mind of Jesus.

The Upper Room Setting

After arriving in Jerusalem, Jesus and the apostles went to an upper room to eat the Passover meal. Jesus washed the feet of the apostles, making a gesture of hospitality usually performed by a slave and teaching them by means of this symbolic action about his servant leadership. While Jesus ate the Passover meal with the apostles, he taught them. He gave them an answer to their inward question of what was on his mind. He told them, "I am with you only a little longer" (John 13:33). He talked about his imminent death. It meant that he would be separated from the apostles. Jesus' announcement of his departure disturbed the apostles and they responded to the impending loss with great grief.

Jesus always nurtured his disciples. Many times during his time with them he dealt with their questions, fears, and anxieties. On the night before Jesus died he took the time to help the apostles with their anticipatory grief caused by his anticipated death.

The Upper Room Teachings of Jesus

In chapters 13-16, John recorded Jesus' teachings in the upper room and these teachings were significant for the apostles at this critical point of need in their lives. Jesus' actions with the apostles also serve as a help for anyone at any time he or she is experiencing anticipatory grief.

Some of the feelings after a great loss can be the same feelings present before an impending loss occurs. Typically, the approaching loss can be a grave illness of someone close or it could be an individual in the process of dying. Anxiety, dread, guilt, helplessness, hopelessness and a sense of being overwhelmed can come upon a person anticipating a significant loss. Just as Jesus helped the apostles, he can help anyone facing an impending loss. Observing his actions and applying his techniques will help.

Presence

Notice that Jesus made a strong emphasis on **his continuing presence.** When Jesus spoke about "going away," the apostles immediately said they wanted to go with him. They could not comprehend being absent from Jesus' earthly presence. To help them with their cry of absence, Jesus spoke about his continuing presence with the apostles. "I will not leave you orphaned; I am coming to you" (John 14:18). By his mighty works of healing and redemption he had made a tremendous popular impact on the twelve. He had gathered around himself to share his ministry a little group of followers who never thought of themselves apart from him.

Now Jesus was telling his followers that he would leave them. They would be on their own. How could they possibly carry on without him? It was then that Jesus made the startling announcement of his going away, but far from being an irreparable loss, it would actually be to their advantage. He had come to them from God, yet his earthly presence with them was never intended to be permanent. Now he was returning to the Father, and the Father would send another Representative, one who would remain with them permanently, who would be their constant Companion, carry on the same ministry, recall to them everything he had taught them, lead them to a mature understanding of the Christian truth, and fortify them in their Christian witness.

"I am coming to you" (John 14:18). He spoke of the coming of the Holy Spirit. He would continue to be present with his followers in another way. He would not be with them in a physical presence but in a spiritual presence. When Christ promised the Spirit, he promised not an energy or a power but a Person, invisible, yet not less real than himself. Where was God when the apostles hurt? He was with them, and he would continue to be with them. Where is God when we hurt today? He is present with us. He "abides" with us, and his followers need to recognize and celebrate his presence.

Years ago when I served as a pastor, I went to the emergency room with a young girl hurt in a go-cart accident in our church parking lot. Her injuries were not life threatening but were quite painful. I called her mother and told her to meet us in the emergency room. As the doctors and other medical personnel treated the young girl, she screamed and cried. I tried to speak comforting words to her. But, she continued to scream and cry when the doctor touched her and when I talked to her. After a short time, the mother arrived in the emergency room and came to her daughter's bed side. The doctors continued the treatment. The girl continued to cry and scream. But, the mother quietly assured her daughter, "Sonya, I am here. Sonya, I am here." The words from that mother quietened the cries of the young girl. Her mother just kept assuring her daughter of her presence. In our cries of hurt, we need to hear Jesus' words, "I am here."

As persons anticipate great loss they should draw on the promise of Jesus, "I am coming to you." He is with us in all of life's difficulties. Nothing brings greater comfort than the reality of presence. Wayne E. Oates wrote that the main purpose of pastoral counseling should be to help people become aware of the majestic presence of God in their lives.[1]

Listening

Notice, also, that **Jesus listened to what his apostles had to say**. He heard their words of resentment about him leaving them, but he did not reprimand them for this resentment. He listened. He heard their words involving questions and doubts. He heard them when they told him about their fears and anxieties. He did not chastise them for these feelings. As they talked, he did not feel the necessity to talk over their talk. He listened. He never evaluated their conversation as small talk or stupid. He listened. The Lord demonstrated the awesome power of the listening ear.

People anticipating loss might need to talk. They usually need someone to be a sympathetic listener. They do not need pious platitudes or theological evaluations. They just need a good listener. Job's friends came to visit him during his time of great suffering. They wanted to help him. They were with him for seven days and seven nights, sitting with him, ready to listen. But, the friends turned out to be miserable comforters when they offered assessments for the cause of his suffering. Hurting people need someone to listen. What greater listener does a person have than the Lord? Hurting people can pray to the Lord in great honesty and know that God listens to everything said, even complaints.

The apostles sensed Jesus' love and care by his listening. One who listens to another demonstrates interest and care for another individual. The good listener creates a therapeutic moment for a grieving person. Anton Tchekov, the Russian writer, in his book *The Short Stories of Anton Tchekov* wrote a short story entitled "Grief." It is the story of Iona Patapov, a driver of a horse-drawn taxi. Iona tries to tell some of his passengers his story. He begins his story with an army officer, but he would not listen. He begins his story with three young men who were his next passengers. They ignored his speech and talked about the pleasure they had experienced during the evening. He tried to share his story at the end of the day with his fellow taxi drivers. All of them were more interested in playing cards than listening to Anton's story. Patapov finally put his horse in the stall, and he told the story to the horse about his daughter becoming gravely ill during the week and ultimately dying. Patapov then seemed to be satisfied, because the horse appeared to listen and to be interested in his story.

Listening to other hurting persons can be one of our greatest gifts to them. Dietrich Bonhoeffer wrote in *Life Together*, "Christians have forgotten that the ministry of listening has been committed to them by Him who is Himself the great listener and whose work they should share."[2] The first-century poet Seneca expressed the age-old desire for a person to listen:

> *Listen to me for a day—an hour—a moment!*
> *Lest I expire in my terrible wilderness, my lonely silence!*
> *O God, is there no one to listen?*

Where was God when the disciples grieved over Jesus' impending death? He was there listening. God's grieving people are not left alone in the dark night of the soul. God is in the darkness to hear our fears of the darkness approaching and, yes, even in our cursing of the coming darkness.

Speaking helpfully

Notice that **Jesus also spoke** words to the apostles who were anxious about his departure. The Lord's word did not involve trite sayings, false promises, worn clichés, or religious slogans. His words created the possibility of comfort. He spoke living, relevant words. These words penetrated into the innermost being of the apostles and gave them comfort and hope.

Words do not have to be meaningless or empty. Words spoken to people in anticipatory grief can be therapeutic and helpful. They can be powerful instruments to help hurting people. Unfortunately, some people speak vain words that add to the hurt of hurting people: "Do not worry, everything is going to be fine." "It is God's will to teach you something." Some people even promise miraculous deliverance from an impending hurt. Miracles do happen, but we need to be careful and realize that God does not respond to every hurt with a miracle, for then we would have a perfect world.

Maybe we can find help for speaking to grieving people by examining what Jesus said to his apostles. The Lord noticed the troubled look on the faces of these men. Then, he spoke gently to them, "Do not let your hearts be troubled. Believe in God, believe also in me" (14:1). He encouraged the apostles to believe. Jesus urged them to believe both in God and in himself. By faith their world that seemed so empty without him would become a place with many rooms. Jesus knew that faith—openness to him—would help them with their hurt.

Jesus also spoke a word about the teaching ministry of the Holy Spirit. "But the Advocate, the Holy Spirit, whom the Father will send in my name will teach you everything" (14:25). The word "everything" involved many dimensions of instruction. Of course, it means teaching the disciples in the way of obedience. But, it also could mean teaching disciples how to cope with human hurts and how to learn from the hurtful experiences of life. With these words Jesus promised his disciples how to endure and even to grow from hurts. To those who believe in Jesus as Lord and Savior, Christ has bequeathed a Spirit of Truth. Believers have a Teacher who trains and interprets life experiences from a divine perspective. As difficulties arise they have to be taught by the Spirit.

Jesus spoke words about believing and about being taught, but he also spoke words about peace. He said to the apostles, "Peace I leave with you; my peace I give to you. I do not give to you as the world gives" (John 14:27). This statement represented strange words coming from a man who stood in a situation that was anything but peaceful. Outside the walls of that upper room a raging, hostile crowd threatened to batter the breath out of his body. Inside that room the hearts of the apostles pounded with fear.

Jesus spoke about the peace he had and could give to others. It involved an inner harmony and well-being that is quite independent of outward circumstances. Of all the qualities of the Master's character, none was more evident than his poise, his marvelous ability to remain calm and serene and self-controlled amid the storms of a boisterous world. Christ offers to his followers that same kind of peace. He is not talking about some psychological mind game. He is talking about a quality of life that he is willing to give to people who receive it.

Conclusion

Christians inevitably face impending crises in life. Sometimes the coming crisis overwhelms them. They have fears. They ask hard questions such as, "Where is God when I hurt?"

Like the apostles, they feel an absence. Maybe the greatest written work on anticipatory grief comes from John chapters 13-16. Hurting people find an answer to their question. They learn from the discourse in the upper room that God is present with his people in his Holy Spirit in every experience of life. They are not alone. They can sense his presence. They also feel confident that they can vent their honest feelings to God in prayer, and he listens. Reading and meditating on the words of Jesus to the apostles inspires faith, encourages learning from the teaching of the Holy Spirit, and draws upon the promise of peace. What a joy to know that Jesus helps us before a sad event occurs!

Notes

[1]Wayne E. Oates, *The Presence of God in Pastoral Counseling* (Waco, TX: Word Books, 1986), 9.

[2]Dietrich Bonhoeffer, *Life Together* (New York: Harper and Row, 1954), 98-99.

The Path to God's Peace in Traumatic Loss: Suggestions for Ministering

J. Donald Smith, Psy. D.
President, Radio Bible Hour and
Good Neighbor International
Sponsor of the J. Harold Smith Pastor Training Center
Carson-Newman College

> *Unless you, too, have lost a child, you cannot begin to know this kind of pain. There is something so wrong about having your child to die before you do; the "order" of the world would have us to believe that children bury their parents. But there I was on April 11th, burying my only son; putting all my hopes and dreams down into the earth in a casket that had to be specially ordered because even undertakers do not count much on four-year-old children dying.*[1]

THOSE WORDS WERE WRITTEN BY MY father, J. Harold Smith, in 1981, about the death in 1942 of his four year old son, J. Harold Smith, Jr. They capture my parent's anguish in the death of a child. Even for a strong Christian like my father, such an experience can shatter every assumption about how the world works, and who God is. Death is a part of the natural (fallen) world. People die, and although we grieve, we accept certain types of death as part of the natural order (We live, we age, we get sick, and eventually, almost as a relief, we die). Although every death of a loved one causes pain for the family, it does not challenge our core beliefs in the way a traumatic loss can. We assume that our parents will die before we do. We assume that we will outlive our children. We assume, perhaps, that because we are faithful people, that we will somehow be protected from the most horrible of life's tragedies. Then, suddenly, there we are, or there is the one we love, encompassed in the terror which we have always quietly dreaded.

Every pastor, and every Christian, will eventually be faced with a traumatic loss within the congregation. Within every community of believers there are people who are enduring traumatic loss. The violent deaths of children, the sudden loss of the life of a loved one through illness or accident, and the ever-increasing loss of life from substance abuse, are a few of the situations that are likely to face the faith community. When a parent or family member is faced with this kind of loss, the effects can be catastrophic for the individual and the family. Faith in God's benevolence can be brought into question and even belief in God can be deeply undermined. These sorts of events are personal, family, and community catastrophes. Individual Christians, pastors, and the church can be critical elements in ministering to those who are suffering through these ordeals.

Reflecting on the Stages of Grief

Elisabeth Kubler-Ross provided a description of the process of facing loss.[2] Her work involved people who had been diagnosed with terminal illness, but her model has been generalized to other grief situations. She proposed five "stages" of grief, and considered that they were sequential and universal. The stages were labeled as Denial, Anger, Bargaining, Depression, and Acceptance. Psychologists no longer see her five stages as sequential because they may occur in no particular order and may recur through the process. But it is generally accepted that these labels can help us understand grief. For the purposes of this discussion we will also consider the role of guilt in the bereaved, and the important role of the quest for some cognitive and spiritual understanding of the event.

A century ago, particularly in rural cultures, the family prepared the deceased for burial, and perhaps interred the body on the family's property. Our culture exposes us to extreme violence and death in its entertainment media, but shields us from death and violence in real life so that it is easy to be numbed to the reality of our mortality. We may assume that the world is relatively safe, or that it cannot happen in our family. When it does happen, it can feel as if the foundations of our lives have suddenly crumbled. For the one facing this kind of loss, there is an immediate sense of unreality. It feels like a horrible dream.

Expressing denial

Hear my father as he describes the early afternoon when he entered that awful ordeal:

> *Myrtice (my wife) and I had gone to the office in downtown Greenville (South Carolina) that day in March when the phone rang, and the voice on the other end shrieked, "Come home! Your son has been burned to death." My son? What were these people saying? Surely there was some mistake.*[3]

Surely there must be some mistake! The report could not be true. The words did not seem to make sense. With the first of such news, a human's insulating barrier begins to emerge, and it is merciful that it does so. One's body feels as if it is failing. It can be described as a feeling of disintegrating. Nausea is common, as is a racing heart; the feeling of dread competes against a desperate hope that this thing might not be so. This dreamlike feeling of unreality may persist for days or weeks after the trauma. It allows one to continue to go through the motions of daily life, and perhaps get through the social obligations of a funeral and all the decisions that have to be made in the immediate aftermath. But denial is denial of reality, and reality is persistent and intrusive. Denial begins to give way to the awful truth that this experience is not a dream. There is a growing dread that one is about to be launched into a world of pain unlike anything ever known before.

Recognizing reality and losing control

> *But it was no mistake. As Sunny was riding his tricycle around on the front porch, the little boy from next door came over and dropped a match into a can which contained just a handful of gasoline . . . Sunny received the full force of the blast. The next few weeks . . . the next twenty-eight days to be exact . . . were torturous to me. I watched his slow dying . . . I watched this beautiful child, horribly burned in a senseless accident, lie in the bed with severe burns on two-thirds of his body . . . he would smile when he awoke and saw me there. I saw his body disintegrate before my eyes . . . .*[4]

Gradually, reality replaces denial and is accompanied by a fear of total collapse. "I cannot bear this," is an expression of the fear of losing control, of "going crazy," of being pushed to the very edge of the ability to continue to function. Faced with a personal tragedy, we are reminded of our own helplessness, and as grief begins to come in waves, "like the sea billows roll," the pain can seem literally unbearable. Spouses and parents are keenly aware of each other's grief, and the grief of surviving family members, and they may start to try to hold it together. Attempts to "stay strong" for others only adds to the already impossible burden.

At the beginning, as one becomes aware of the loss, denial helps to soften the shock. The experience is one of numbness, alternating with acute psychological pain as the reality emerges. There may be perceptual distortion or extreme disorientation. The person in grief will want information about what has occurred, but should not be flooded with grim details surrounding the death, if possible. It is a time for helpers to be present, and responsive, and to help with practical decision-making as necessary. It is not a time to ask, "How are you feeling?" It is not a time to talk in platitudes, such as "She is in a better place," or even "We'll see him again." Platitudes will not work. For those who want to help, simple expressions of sorrow are best and finding ways to be useful by running errands, or providing food for the family is important. Being gently present is what is most helpful at this early stage, and throughout the process.

Expressing anger

Anger is also a normal aspect of grief. It is natural to want someone to blame when we are hurting. Anger may be directed toward those who are perceived to be responsible, and sometimes at any other person in proximity, including caregivers. Anger toward God is not unusual, and the pastor may be the focus of that anger. It is important for caregivers to recognize that this anger is part of an adaptive process. It is an attempt to begin to make sense of what has happened. It is important to hear the anger and acknowledge it, but not to confront it. If possible, anger should not be taken personally, although it may be expressed very personally. Depending on the circumstances, anger may focus on the perceived cause of the death, such as a drunk driver, or a drug dealer, or even on the spouse or other family member who may have been present at the time of death (and failed to prevent the tragedy). Occasionally the anger focuses on the deceased. It is important that one should not be shocked by any expression of anger, but support and try to understand the anger as part of the grief work.

In my clinical practice, I was asked to see a woman whose husband of more than forty years had suddenly died two years earlier. She had obvious symptoms of agitated depression, and was still struggling to adapt to her husband's death. As she described her life to me, it was clear that she was seething with anger. When her husband had died, she did not know how to write a check, or how to manage the household utilities. She did not know how to fill the car with gas. Her husband had done all these things for her, and she felt as if she were an abandoned child. Although his intentions had been good, he had left her dependent, alone, and resentful. My role involved getting her to express all the feelings she was having, and not just the sadness. Expressing anger at the deceased is not socially acceptable, but the feelings may be very real and should not be ignored. The person in grief may oscillate between feeling angry and feeling guilty about being angry. As I reassured her that those feelings were normal and not unusual, she was able to put them into words, and accept them. Within two weeks she was sleeping well, her depression had alleviated, and she was working toward resolving and managing her grief more effectively.

I rehearse this case in order to remind caregivers that some feelings, especially of anger at the deceased, may be operating just below the conscious level. Such may be true in cases where the deceased may have been compliant in his or her own death, as for example, in a suicide, or drug-related overdose death, or in situations where the death was caused by some reckless act on the part of the deceased. These feelings may be very strong and are very common.

With respect to anger toward God, the church community should remain loving and gentle, and be the instrument of the expression of God's love toward the bereaved. These events will have an effect on faith. For some, tragic loss leads to an abandonment of faith, and the beginning of a period of rebellion against God. On the other hand, the experience of the tragedy can become a rock-solid foundation on which a deeper and stronger faith is built. My experience is that when renewed faith is the outcome, it is largely because of the persistent and gentle love of the Christian community, and not primarily because of good arguments and solid reasons why God should be trusted (although these will have their place at a later time).

Threatening our faith

> *. . . I hit bottom in March of 1942. At that time I received the heaviest blow of my personal life, and I met head on what I would honestly call the lowest ebb*

> *of my ministry. The temptation came to lose my belief in God, to feel He had failed me, when I was going all over the country, night and day, preaching and doing my best for Him. It seemed the Devil said, "Now, see how God pays you off. Quit preaching. Give up. Deny your faith."*[5]

For the Christian who is challenged by this kind of loss, there is a profound and realistic fear that our faith will not hold. When we face the extreme test of faith, because it is a test, we fear we might fail. Extreme loss is an extreme risk for our spiritual lives. It confronts us with the evil in the world. It confronts us with the fact that God does not always shelter us from experiencing genuine horror. It confronts us with the truth that when we love, we expose ourselves to almost unbearable pain. What if I lost my belief that God is really my ally, that he really loves me? What if, in this grief, I came to believe God no longer was a loving God, or even that he did not exist? There is an existential threat to our faith that these situations pose.

Some will be lost to the Christian community, and will lose the joy of their salvation, but I do not believe they will be lost to God. Our salvation is sealed by the Holy Spirit, and not by our will, or our ability to endure trauma. But the risk is still there, that we will lose the joy of fellowship with Christ, and with fellow believers, and if that happens, our best chance for an abundant life beyond this tragedy will be lost.

Withdrawing from relationships

Because of the loss of a dear loved one, some will attempt to withdraw from other loving relationships, for fear of losing those also. The death of a child puts an enormous stress on marriages and families. Many divorces follow the loss of a child. Sometimes one spouse will harbor feelings of blame and anger toward the spouse after the loss. Other children will be impacted, not just with their own grief, but with the response of the parents to the surviving children. Often parents become obsessively concerned with the safety of the surviving children. One dear friend described how, after the death of one of his sons, he became known to his children as "Mr. Safety" as he attempted to protect them from every conceivable risk. The community of helpers should recognize that after traumatic loss, loving and supporting the whole family is needed.

A most important quality which helpers will need is patience. Healing takes time, and help may not be welcomed at first. Even if the bereaved person stops attending church, or withdraws from friends, it is critical to recognize that the anger inherent in the grief process is not the final word. Keep reaching out to the suffering in patient but persistent kindness. Kindness, prayerfully offered, is a very powerful form of God's love.

Bargaining and guilt

Kubler-Ross's stage of bargaining is less relevant in cases of sudden traumatic death, but is very real when the family member is injured or has somehow survived the initial injury. More important and closely tied to this process of bargaining is the very significant problem of guilt. "If I had only lived my life differently, this tragedy would not have happened. So if he/she can survive, I'll make the changes." When the death occurs, there are likely to be some significant feelings of guilt. They may be rational or irrational. In traumatic loss, particularly of children, survivors will certainly begin to ask how this horror might have been avoided. For my parents the fact that they were not at home when the tragedy occurred tormented them, even though the child had been left in competent care. Most of these guilt-inducing "what-ifs" are not rational, but they are very predictable and must eventually be addressed. It is important for caregivers not to minimize these feelings. They should be acknowledged, but then addressed rationally. For example, "I know you feel you could have prevented this event if you had been at home, but the need to provide for your family requires that you be at work." "You could not have known this tragedy would have happened on that day at that time. You could not just stop working to be with the child around the clock." Reason is powerful against irrational guilt.

Parents, and particularly Christian parents, accept the responsibility for protecting their children from danger. If the child dies traumatically, they are likely to feel that they have failed somehow. The feelings of helplessness and impotence in carrying out this responsibility give rise to guilt that can be very crippling. Occasionally a parent is an immediate cause; for example, the parent who is driving when a deadly accident occurs. It is important for the parent eventually to work through that guilt and to recognize his or her intention was not to injure or hurt his or her child. Again, they must eventually recognize that one cannot possibly protect a child from every danger, or even from most dangers.

In the case of a death for which one is morally responsible, for example a parent who is driving while intoxicated, and a child dies as a result, it is a different matter. Where there is reasonable justification for believing one has caused a death through negligence or selfishness, guilt is the appropriate response, and confession and repentance are necessary for healing. This kind of healing requires supernatural intervention, but it is the sort of situation where Christ's atonement and forgiveness can become graciously effective.

Depression

As one begins to accept the loss that has occurred, Kubler-Ross noted that depression is to be expected. A loss of energy, and appetite, feelings of hopelessness and sadness predominate and may result in clinical depression if it persists. It is not abnormal for these feelings to persist for a year or more. If the ability to resume other responsibilities is seriously impacted, or if the depression is leading to other problems, such as serious weight loss or gain, or prolonged insomnia, it may be necessary to seek medical advice. There may be an increased risk for suicide or other injurious behavior such as substance abuse during the process. Obviously these kinds of developments require professional attention. Nearly everyone who goes through this process, however, will experience a long period of heartache, which gradually gets better over time.

In this period of gradual improvement, there are occasions when the tragedy is brought back in full force. Birthdays, special holidays and other marker dates may lead to a re-emergence of these feelings for years afterwards. Although this return of symptoms may seem to be disturbing to others, it is at the core of the grieving process. This period of generalized depression is the darkness before the dawn. Even as it begins to lift, it can unexpectedly get very dark again.

Other reactions

During this time, life may seem largely bleak and barren. The loss of the ability to experience pleasure (anhedonia) is common. Food loses its taste, entertainments seem empty, and even words intended for spiritual comfort may seem meaningless, inauthentic, and hollow. The world seems lifeless, painted in shades of gray. There are constant unavoidable reminders of the loss. The empty place at the dinner table, the toys, the little shoes, the room that is empty, generate renewed pain. There may be feelings of envy toward those who are not experiencing loss. Parents who lose children report feelings of resentment when they see another family happily enjoying their time together. Tears seem to come at inappropriate times and in response to seemingly irrelevant stimuli. Fear of losing emotional control may isolate a person at home. Close friends are so important at this time, and they should reassure the grieving friend that "crying is okay."

Caring for the Grieving

Grieving is a time for regular pastoral contact and support. Grieving support groups are also very important and helpful, as are on-line support groups which have emerged in the last decade.

The importance of presence

Pastors and other caregivers are often reluctant to be with those who are deeply wounded, thinking that they need to be prepared to say something helpful. Feeling helpless in the face of this kind of trauma is normal, and almost universal. Helpers should be reassured that nothing needs to be said. Nothing in particular needs to be done, except just to be present or available. The grieving person has gone through something unusual, and friends may feel that because they have not experienced this kind of loss for themselves, that they cannot be helpful. Although someone with a similar loss can be especially credible, any caring friend can still be a blessing. What helps is being willing to go to the home, spend time with the grieving person, help out in little tasks, and be ready to listen when the time is right. If possible, healthy lifestyle choices in diet and vigorous exercise can shorten the period of depression.

The significance of compassion in care giving

It is important to remember what the person has suffered, and to realize that only God can really mend this broken spirit. There is no magical action, no "just right" word of comfort, powerful enough to fix this kind of grief. Psychological trauma is akin to a physical wound. It will take time to become bearable, and it will not be mended by any particular word or action. In my father's experience, however, he found small signs of compassion to be comforting.

> *As I was standing in the receiving line at the funeral, a lady walked up and took my hand. She did not say anything at first, but as she stood there for a few moments, a tear fell from her eye onto my hand. Then she said, "I had a son who was burned to death." I tell you the truth; that tear did more to comfort me than all the flowers and anything else that anyone said. At that moment, I experienced a peace I had not known before.*[6]

Those who have themselves endured this kind of tragedy, and who have found a way to survive and grow in faith through the experience, can be enormously helpful. Thousands of people came by the home or came to the funeral and expressed their sympathy, but it was the lady's tear on his hand that my father remembered most vividly fifty years later, and that brought him immediate comfort. For the one who endures the tragedy, the developing awareness that they have a ministry gift to offer can be a marker on the pathway to finding meaning in the disaster. The ability to bring any measure of comfort in the middle of devastation is no small gift!

The search for meaning

As part of the healing process, the search for a meaningful understanding of the events will occur. We need to be able to integrate what has happened into the larger understanding of ourselves, our world, and our God. The search for meaning is part of what is required to live fully beyond the trauma. The explanation and understanding does not have to be complete and comprehensive. It is more like a good working hypothesis, a tentative and open-ended explanation that seems to fit the experience. Here is my father again, sharing some of what he had learned.

> *One of the things I will never do is "explain" why God took my son. I know there were powerful lessons in this experience for me to learn . . . I learned what it was to feel with others to whom I have ministered in times of loss. Maybe this is when I really learned to trust Him. Through the years of World War II, and the wars in Korea and Viet Nam, I ministered to many families who had lost sons. I learned something about God's heart, knowing that He, too, had lost His Son.*[7]

The quest to make sense of it all is an important part of the grief work. It cannot be rushed, and it is an intensely personal task. As a caregiver you cannot meaningfully tell the person in grief what it all means. The temptation to do so will be great. As helpers, we want to help; we want to be effective. Wonderful life lessons may seem obvious to us from the outside, but if we offer them to the person in acute grief, they are likely to seem trivial and irrelevant, and are more likely to provoke anger than healing. The meaning of the catastrophe will be shaped by the response to it, and must be personally discovered.

We must respect the fact that God is at work in the life of the grieving individual, and we can trust Him. I have found that during this time in the recovery, there is an openness on the part of people to reading and hearing messages if they deal profoundly with issues like the sovereignty of God, and the problem of evil. These means can often be powerful tools in rebuilding the wounded psyche.

> *What I am describing is very painful for me . . . this was the first big loss of my life, and as I relive the experience, I am aware of a sadness it left in me, a sadness I could endure only because I finally felt underneath me, supporting me, providing for me in the dark night of personal despair, a very amazing grace . . . the everlasting arms of One who had suffered more.*[8]

It takes time!

Although my parents learned to live and eventually laugh again, there was always a place of sadness in their hearts. For my father, the sadness was there until a few weeks before his death, and then it began to change. In the weeks before my father died at the age of 91, tears came to his eyes as he spoke of the death of Sunny, and how much he anticipated their reunion in Christ. As he got closer to death, that wounded place in him that always felt heavy and bleak, was starting to be transformed into something that I could only describe as anticipatory joy. In working with unresolved grief, I have come to believe that these traumas never completely disappear. It is completely normal for a parent to shed tears half a century later for a lost child. But for the Christian, the Blessed Hope is powerful and transformational as the ultimate resolution of all grief.

In time the burden becomes bearable, and there are more and more moments of respite from the anguish. Some have told me they were surprised to find themselves laughing after days, or weeks or months with no glimmer of joy. Invariably, that laughter was followed by feelings of guilt, as if they were somehow dishonoring the missing one. Assurance that it is both good and right to resume life, and to find new joy in life, is a message that the caregiver can share.

Grief can be compartmentalized and managed more easily as the healing continues. I have sometimes suggested that when feelings of sadness come at inappropriate times, that one should make an appointment to grieve at a particular later time. Everyone is unique, and for some these formal times, such as visits to a gravesite or a favorite place can be helpful. For others, these options may not seem to be valid. Each person will find his or her own way.

As time goes by, the darkness continues to lift, and color returns to life. Those who go through this experience are changed by it. I am struck by the parallels in the changes that cancer survivors and survivors of traumatic loss experience. Life does not seem the same, ever again. Nothing is taken for granted; relationships have a new richness and a new urgency.

Perspective is restored and priorities are rearranged. Material things never mean as much, and each day is seen as a gift. On the other hand, there is a loss of innocence: The worst can happen, and it can happen to me. Gone is the blissful ignorance, and delusions of adolescent immortality, and in its place something more wise and less comfortable. For many, both cancer and traumatic loss are experienced as the beginning of a more genuine life, a truly spiritual life, and a more authentic way of being in the world.

The way of peace

For the Christian there is the mystical supernatural irrational "peace that passes understanding." I love that expression. It is just simply perfect. It is the peace that makes no sense, but it is greater than reason. It encompasses reason, is above reason, and becomes sufficient to let the rational mind rest. Since the trauma, the mind has not stopped trying to get answers, spinning, careening, almost out of control at times. But God's peace runs past and catches that troubled mind in its arms, and says, "Even in this, all is well."

God's peace is a holy gift to those who suffer. It is what we should pray for when we suffer. And when we seek to help those who suffer, it is what we should pray to give. We never can be sure when God will allow us to minister to those who suffer. But we must be willing to go, to be with the suffering. When that wonderful lady came to my brother's funeral, it must have been hard for her. It would have reminded her of her own loss. It would have been painful to open her wounds again, and see our suffering family, the flowers and the coffin. But she came, with tears in her eyes, and took my father's hand, and she brought the gift of the peace of God.

Conclusion

All of us are on this glorious, sometimes terrifying journey. For some, Jesus Christ has come and offered the gift of himself and we have accepted his offer. We have the promise that all that happens will work together for good (for the glory of God.) Our task is simple, but in times of loss, very difficult, and that task is to trust our Lord to be sufficient. As humans, we have nothing our God needs. But somehow, our Lord is pleased by our faith and trust. In a way, it is all we have to offer. When our deepest fears have become real, and we lie crushed and broken in the dark prison of grief, and we can still lift our eyes toward God, and say with our dear and most precious Christ, "Not my will, but Thine be done," we fulfill our reason for being, and we can discover the peace that passes understanding. In our deepest loss, we discover our greatest opportunity to trust our God most deeply, and to express our ultimate satisfaction in Him. For pastors and fellow Christians, that is where we want to be, and that is where we want those who suffer to arrive.

> *And I learned that I can find a way to sing from the dark prison of despair . . . .*[9]

Final Word

I would like to say thanks to the authors of the other chapters in this book.

Their writings here are acts of personal and spiritual bravery. I admire them for their courage in writing. For many of my fellow writers, I know this experience had to be painful; it would have opened wounds that are perhaps never fully healed in this life. That God would arrange to have so many gifted, wounded, and faithful souls gather in the School of Religion of Carson-Newman is, I believe, supernatural. Like that sweet woman who carried her own burden, but still chose to come and offer comfort at my brother's funeral, my prayer is that you will be rewarded by knowing that your work will inspire, encourage, and help bring God's peace to many who are walking where you have already walked. I consider it a blessing and a great honor to be in such company.

Notes

[1]J. Harold Smith, *Time of My Life* (Orlando: Radio Bible Hour, 1981), 44.

[2]Elisabeth Kubler-Ross, *On Death and Dying* (New York: MacMillan Co., 1969).

[3]Smith, *Time of My Life*, 45.

[4]Smith, *Time of My Life*, 46.

[5]Smith, *Time of my Life*, 44.

[6]J. Harold Smith, *My Life for the Lord.* An Audio Recording (Radio Bible Hour, Inc., 1995).

[7] Smith, *Time of My Life*, 44.

[8] *Ibid.*

[9] *Ibid.*

CONCLUSION

IN *AUTHENTIC CHRISTIANITY* JOHN STOTT described death and nothingness in the following way:

> *Nothing baffles us human beings more than nothingness and death. The 'angst' of . . . existentialists is . . . their dread of the abyss of nothingness. And death is the one event over which (in the end) we have no control, and from which we cannot escape . . . But nothingness and death are no problem to God.*[1]

This present book has been written in an honest effort on the part of the authors and the editors to face the great angst which challenges all of us as mortals. We have not sought to hide the horrendous journey through which we travel in relation to death and grief. Some readers may be offended by the fact that we have not run this course with easy clichés or tried to cover up our exhausting wrestling matches with the ultimate reality of humanity in the death of those who are our loved ones. We have not provided so-called Christian platitudes of superficial hope in the midst of our genuine grief. Death is a real enemy (1 Cor 15:26) and we as humans do not handle death very well.

We may be healed by the sweet touch of our caring Lord and our loving Christian families in our communities of faith who have stood with us in this healing process. Nevertheless, the wounds are still there and the pain will not be totally removed until we stand before our Lord at the *eschaton* of newness in heaven and then finally realize that in all authenticity our tears have been wiped away and our pain has been terminated (Rev 21:3-5). Such a resolution is our God-given hope which is sealed to us in the resurrection of Jesus and guaranteed through the presence of the Holy Spirit in our current lives (cf. Eph 1:14; 2 Cor 1:22; 5:5).

Those who have walked through the Valley of the Shadow of Death with a loved one know that it is a heart wrenching experience, the results of which are not integrated into our lives quickly. It takes time to absorb such traumas and become physically, psychologically and spiritually realigned so that we re-enter the disciplines of life and become reestablished in a wholesome manner.

In the process of facing death and grief I would hesitatingly share with you two diagrammatic illustrations which were given to me by my friend and former colleague, the late Wayne E. Oates, for whom another colleague Andrew E. Lester and I edited his *festschrift*.[2]

These two diagrams for dealing with grief have stuck with me and I have used them on countless occasions in dealing with the bereaved. I share them with you now in the hope that you will be able to use them when you are seeking to help others who are struggling with grief or if and when you yourself may be faced with such an encounter. They are not meant to be used haphazardly but at a time when the grieving person is actually ready to listen. I admit that I have sometimes used them too soon and the person was not ready to listen.

The first illustration comes from the time when I was a doctoral student at Princeton and Wayne was on leave, teaching and studying there. In a conversation with him on grief and trauma, he diagramed for me the picture of a narrow road on which you are driving and as you are coming down a steep hill there is a narrow bridge at the bottom of the ravine. Unfortunately, you see a huge truck coming down the road on the other side of the ravine. You know instinctively that you will both meet on the narrow bridge and you are convinced that you will not be able to pass adequately on the bridge but there is nothing you can do except go forward. Well, as you guessed, you were able to pass each other but in the process you are shaken because your psyche was left behind up the hill. So what you then do is to pull over to the side of the road and "re-live" the experience. But you do so over and over again. When you have done so for a sufficient number of times and convinced yourself that you have come through the episode, you can restart your journey and continue on your way.

Wayne then said to me that a person going through grief must "re-live" and "re-tell" the story over and over again until the grieving person can resume the journey. That re-telling may take months and years. And he added, as ministers we need to help grieving people find others to whom they can tell and re-tell their stories. In the re-telling of the story comes a sense of healing. Patience on the part of a listening friend or caregiver is one of the greatest gifts one can offer to anyone in the turmoil of grief.

The second illustration came to me when we were colleagues in Louisville and I had just lost my mother in death. As Wayne and I sat at lunch, he took out a napkin and drew a type of pie having various sized pieces, some very large, some medium sized, and some much smaller. Then he said to me: "Jerry, this pie represents your relationships." When a small piece is removed, it does not affect the rest of the pie very much and it is easy to adjust the remaining pieces of the pie to fill up the empty space. But when a big piece is removed, then all the rest of the pieces in the pie become unglued and very loose. The stability of the entire pie is threatened. For the pie to become stable again, requires the other pieces to grow larger and for new pieces to be slowly added to the pie. The temptation, in the case of losing a spouse for example, is to try to insert another piece into the pie too quickly and it usually does not fit or work very well. The pie has to re-grow its pieces naturally. Otherwise, there will be continuing trauma which results when mourning has not taken place adequately. Believe me, I have witnessed a number of cases where mourning did not adequately take place and the pie did not readjust.

Now while losing a spouse can be very traumatic for the bereaved, losing a child can often be even more traumatic. The option of any future replacement is not really even possible, even though one may have additional children. Therefore, the grief can continue to fester or return long after the death has occurred.

Family, friends and caregivers should try to understand the nature of such grief and provide support and space in such situations. In these articles you should have sensed the need for a gentle listening presence to be offered to the bereaved whether it is a parent, a spouse or a friend. Such a listening presence can be a great solace to a grieving person. The scar from such a death of a child is especially very deep because it is not what we can easily rationalize as a natural human order to life. Yet scarred healing is still possible with God. In this process the love and understanding of fellow Christians is one of the great gifts that God has given to humans in establishing the church–the community of faith.

In spite of all the traumas of life, however, the assault of death and grieving upon humans is not the final word of Scripture. The coming to wholeness (salvation) is the enduring message of God for humanity. God has indeed sought constantly to bring humans to wholeness. Such is the repeated message of the Bible from Genesis to Revelation. Moreover, God has also suffered the trauma of losing a son in the torturous death of Jesus. God knows what such a loss means and God does not forget what such a loss implies. In the darkness of divine grief, God acted with power in the resurrection of Jesus. And for the followers of God's son, Jesus supplied a strategic word of hope. He knew that in the context of the created world we would most certainly experience not only death and evil but even outright hostility and persecution. Nevertheless, he also proclaimed with resolute assurance that we should be confident in the face of such a traumatic world setting because he truly knows our pains and suffering and he has "overcome" this world's evil onslaughts (John 16:33).

As we look to the future, we often see only dimly the hope that is in front of us (1 Cor 13:12) and many times we do so with very tear-filled eyes. But the living Christ has promised to be with us throughout all of life (Matt 28:20). In this mortal life our children may become orphaned by human parents, and parents or spouses may lose their offspring or partners in natural or tragic circumstances, but Jesus will never leave us orphaned and devoid of divine direction (John 14:18).

The conclusion to our stories and to all of history has already been written at the cross when Jesus gasped that "It is finished!" (John 19:20). Those same words have reverberated far beyond the cross and are encapsulated not only in John's visions concerning the coming judgment on evil (Rev 16:17), but also in his vision of the new heaven and the new earth (Rev 21:6). We may struggle with the harshness of this life but our hope is secure in the Son of God who suffered, died and rose again to make us whole. Living out that confession is the foundation for authentic Christianity, even in the context of brutal pain and suffering.

May God who sent a living message in Christ Jesus give to everyone who suffers the assault of grief a vital sense of the dynamic hope that was proclaimed in the resurrection of Jesus and has been made available freely to all who accept that divine invitation.

Notes

[1]John Stott, *Authentic Christianity from the Writings of John Stott*, ed. Timothy Dudley-Smith (Downers Grove, IL, InterVarsity Press, 1995), 393.

[2]See Gerald L. Borchert and Andrew D. Lester, eds., *Spiritual Dimensions of Pastoral Care: Witness to the Ministry of Wayne E. Oates* (Philadelphia: Westminster Press, 1985).

G. L. B. (Co-Editor)

Selected Readings on Grief and Pain: An Annotated Bibliography

Editor's Note: The source of the annotation is given in brackets at the end of each entry.

Aden, Leroy H. and Robert G. Hughes. *Preaching God's Compassion: Comforting Those Who Suffer.* (Fortress Press, 2009). Centering on five particular situations of suffering—loss, illness, violence, fear, and failure—the book suggests ways in which the pastor can preach to parishioners who are experiencing one or more of these traumas. The co-authors are seminary professors of pastoral care and preaching, respectively. [Amazon.com]

Boyd, Gregory A. *Is God to Blame? Beyond Pat Answers to the Problem of Suffering.* (InterVarsity, 2003).
Boyd, a professor-turned-pastor, takes direct aim at a theology that holds that God causes evil and tragedy. Boyd argues for a God who, rather than causing suffering, is in the middle of the fray fighting evil, redeeming suffering, hurting with those of us who hurt, and ultimately defeating that very evil.
[Chad Hartsock]

Brehony, Kathleen A. *After the Darkest Hour: How Suffering Begins the Journey to Wisdom.* (Henry Holt & Co., 2000).
Acknowledging that living brings a variety of losses to the human experience, Brehony sees these experiences of suffering as opportunities for redemption, growth and wisdom. While grief is often associated with death, Brehony widens that understanding of grief, providing suggestions for finding meaning in and though those times. [Carolyn Blevins]

Claypool, John. *The Hopeful Heart.* (Morehouse Publishing, 2003).
Hope is a vital ingredient to the healthy spiritual life, but maintaining hope in the face of disappointments is challenging. Claypool encourages us and inspires us to keep hope alive.
[Don Garner]

Claypool, John. *Mending the Heart.* (Cowley Publications, 1999).
These three meditations, each beginning with a Psalm and ending with a prayer, focus on three common sources of human brokenness—grievance, guilt, and grief. He wrote these profound reflections following the death of his mother.
[Don Garner]

Claypool, John. *Tracks of a Fellow Struggler: How To Handle Grief.* (Word Books, 1975).
These four sermons were preached by this pastor to his church shortly after the death of his ten year-old daughter following a long struggle with leukemia. He concludes that life is a gift and that everything, including grief and gratitude, flow from that fact. The sermons are snapshots of different stages of grief, from the first sermon following the tragedy to one preached several years later. [Chad Hartsock]

Glazer, Rabbi Mel. *And God Created Hope: Finding Your Way through Grief with Lessons from Early Biblical Stories.* (Marlowe, 2007).
Glazer, a certified grief recovery specialist, finds hope for those experiencing grief in stories from Genesis to Lamentations. Glazer combines honesty and hope effectively. [Carolyn Blevins]

James, John W. and Russell Friedman. *The Grief Recovery Handbook, 20th Anniversary Expanded Edition: The Action Program for Moving Beyond Death, Divorce, and Other Losses including Health, Career, and Faith.* (William Morrow Paperbacks, 20th anniversary edition, 2009).
Incomplete recovery from grief can have a lifelong negative effect on the capacity for happiness. Drawing from their own histories as well as from others', the authors illustrate how it is possible to recover from grief and regain energy and spontaneity. Based on a proven program, *The Grief Recovery Handbook* offers grievers the specific actions needed to move beyond loss. [Amazon.com]

Hipps, Richard S., editor. *When A Child Dies: Stories of Survival and Hope.* (Peake Road Books, 1996).
A collection of reports and reflections from ten grieving parents who seek to comfort others with their witness to grief and faith. They speak about the practical questions, emotional afflictions, and spiritual challenges involved in the death of a child.
[Don Garner]

Johnson, L. D. *Morning After Death.* (Broadman Press, 1978).
Writing about the death of his daughter in an automobile accident on the day after her 23rd birthday, this wise professor-chaplain-pastor bears witness to the love of God in the face of evil in our lives. It still stands as a classic statement concerning the treasured beauty of life and the depth of comfort available in the face of death. [Don Garner]

Kushner, Harold. *When Bad Things Happen to Good People.* (Schocken Books, 1981).
This popular best-seller is written in fluid prose by a Jewish rabbi who lost his young son to death from progeria, the accelerated aging disease. His particular approach to suffering and loss is one held by many in our culture who do not bring a resurrection faith to their experience of death. His presentation of some of

the issues may be helpful as we relate to the thoughts, assumptions, and feelings of hurting people. [Don Garner]

Lewis, C. S. *A Grief Observed*. (HarperOne, 2001).
Lewis joined the human race when his wife, Joy Gresham, died of cancer. Lewis, the Oxford don whose Christian apologetics make it seem like he had an answer for everything, experienced crushing doubt for the first time after his wife's tragic death. This book inspired the film *Shadowlands*, but it is more wrenching, more revelatory, and more real than the movie. It is a beautiful and unflinchingly honest record of how even a stalwart believer can lose all sense of meaning in the universe, and how he can gradually regain his bearings.
[Michael Joseph Gross on Amazon.com]

Lewis, C. S. *The Problem of Pain*. (HarperOne, 2001).
Arguing that pain serves a useful and maturing purpose in the life of the believer, Lewis maintains that a life free of suffering that we think we want would not be best for us. [Don Garner]

Lucado, Max. "The Fog of A Broken Heart" in *No Wonder They Call Him the Savior*. (Multnomah Books, 1996; reprint by Thomas Nelson Publishers, 2011).
This insightful meditation on the agony of Jesus in Gethsemane makes the human suffering of Jesus understandable to the hurting person. The fact that God knows our pain can be a deep source of comfort in our own times of crisis. [Don Garner]

Maston, T. B. *God Speaks Through Suffering*. (Word Books, 1978)
The author addresses an age old question about suffering in human experience. From the perspective of his own experience with a son handicapped from birth, Maston offers a pathway of hope and faith for readers who are struggling with their own suffering. [Bill Blevins]

Mitchell, Kenneth R. and Herbert Andersen. *All Our Losses, All Our Griefs: Resources for Pastoral Care.* (Westminster John Knox Press, 1983).
Grief as a lifelong human experience is the scope of this absorbing book. Kenneth Mitchell and Herbert Anderson explore the multiple dimensions of the problem, including the origins and dynamics of grief, loss throughout life, caring for those who grieve, and the theology of grieving. This examination is enriched by vivid illustrations and case histories of individuals whose experiences the authors have shared. [Amazon.com]

Noel, Brook and Pamela D. Blair. *I Wasn't Ready to Say Goodbye: Surviving, Coping and Healing After the Sudden Death of a Loved One.* (Champion, 2000).
A sudden death deprives a family of the goodbyes and presents some unique paths of grief. Brook and Blair address those issues as well as others such as helping children deal with grief. Also included are grief recovery exercises. [Carolyn Blevins]

Nuland, Sherwin B. *How We Die: Reflections of Life's Final Chapter.* (Vintage, 1995).
The author of this best-seller is a Clinical Professor of Surgery at Yale University School of Medicine and a Fellow at Yale's Institute for Social and Policy Studies. Drawing upon his own broad experience and the characteristics of the six most common death-causing diseases, the author examines what death means to the doctor, patient, nurse, administrator, and family.
[William Beatty on Amazon.com]

Oates, Wayne E. *Grief, Transition, and Loss: A Pastor's Practical Guide.* (Augsburg, 1997).

As pastoral counselor and professor, Oates offers guidance to the pastor who is helping others through various experiences of loss and moving forward. [Don Garner]

Prend, Ashley Davis. *Transcending Loss: Understanding the Lifelong Impact of Grief and How to Make It Meaningful.* (Berkley, 1997).
While many authors focus on the immediate impact of grief, Prend focuses on the grief that lingers and lingers and how it changes. As a grief counselor, she suggests ways to become "stronger in the broken places." [Carolyn Blevins]

Schiraldi, Glenn. *A Post-Traumatic Stress Disorder Sourcebook: A Guide to Healing, Recovery, and Growth.* (McGraw-Hill, 2nd Ed, 2009).
The PTSD model can be applied to sudden traumatic loss. This book provides a good overview of the PTSD model, and its implications for increased risk of substance abuse and family disintegration. [Don Smith]

Smith, Harold Ivan. *A Long-Shadowed Grief: Suicide and Its Aftermath.* (Cowley Publications, 2007).
In the aftermath of suicide, friends and family face a long road of grief and reflection. With a sympathetic eye and a firm hand, Harold Ivan Smith searches for the place of the spirit in the wake of suicide. He asks how one may live a spiritual life as a survivor, and he addresses the way faith is permanently altered by "the residue of stigma" that attaches to suicide. [Amazon.com]

Swindoll, Charles R. *Job: A Man of Heroic Endurance*, "Great Lives from God's Word Series, Volume 7." (Thomas Nelson, 2004).
Through tough questions and unexpected answers from God, Job gained new insights on suffering, patience, and endurance.

And, more importantly, he learned how deeply he was loved by God. Swindoll highlights Job's heroic endurance. [Amazon.com]

Weatherhead, Leslie. *The Will of God.* (Abingdon, 1999).
These five sermons were preached in London during the height of World War II, by a kind and thoughtful pastor whose church members faced daily deaths and devastation. This work remains a classic statement of seeking to understand God's presence with us through a crisis. [Don Garner]

Weaver, Andrew J., editor. *Reflections on Grief and Spiritual Growth.* (Abingdon Press, 2005)
Eighteen Christian leaders here contribute personal reflections on their experiences with grief and loss as a part of their faith journey. An included study guide helps individuals and groups grapple with the reality of grief and loss in the context of their Christian faith so that we may better learn to grieve as those who have hope. [Amazon.com]

Westberg, Granger E. *Good Grief*, 50th anniversary edition. (Fortress Press, 2010).
A very brief, easy-to-read treatment of loss and the process of grief, this book can be shared with a person in the first days following loss. It is general enough to relate to any kind of loss. [Don Garner]

Wiersbe, David W. *Gone But Not Lost: Grieving the Death of a Child.* (Baker Books, 2011).
Traumatic loss is considered from the pastor's perspective, with special attention to guilt and marital strain which results from the loss. [Don Smith]

Wiesel, Elie. *Night.* (Bantam Books, 1960).
Wiesel, a concentration camp survivor and 1986 Nobel Peace Prize winner, reflects on his experience as a youth in Auschwitz

and Buchenwald. Terrifying, shocking, and unforgettable, Wiesel's memoir of that experience raises the deepest of questions about God, suffering, justice, and redemption. [Chad Hartsock]

Wiesenthal, Simon. *The Sunflower: On the Possibilities and Limits of Forgiveness.* (Schocken Books, 1969, revised 1997). Wiesenthal is a World War II concentration camp survivor. In this book, more than fifty people respond to the question of tragedy, forgiveness, and theodicy, including theologians, politicians, and world leaders. [Chad Hartsock]

Wolterstorff, Nicholas. *Lament For A Son.* (Eerdmans Publishing Co, 1987).
In deeply personal reflections following the death of his 25 year-old son in a climbing accident in Austria, this seasoned Christian philosopher has voiced the thoughts and feelings of many who grieve a keen loss. With its theological depth and emotional transparency, this book has helped many readers since it first appeared. It is the book I wish I might have written, but I know mine would not be this profound. [Don Garner]

Worden, J. William: *Grief Counseling and Grief Therapy: A Handbook for the Mental Health Practitioner.* (Springer Publishing, 2008).
This text offers an in-depth look at approaches to grief for the professional helper, and is an excellent review of grief counseling. It is widely used for training professionals in the field of grief counseling. [Don Smith]

Wright, N.T. *Evil and the Justice of God.* (InterVarsity, 2006). Wright, one of the world's foremost New Testament scholars, presents a very readable treatment of the question of evil in the world and God's response to it. This work presents deep scholarship in a way that is accessible to ministers, laymen, or even casual theologians. It is required reading for those who want to work out a theology of where God is in tragedy, and to do so in a way that is thoroughly biblical. [Chad Hartsock]

Yancey, Philip. *Disappointment With God: Three Questions No One Asks Aloud.* (Zondervan, 1988).
From the author's Foreward: "Disappointment implies a hoped-for relationship that somehow has not worked out. I am, after all, writing for people who have, at one time or another, heard the silence of God." So three questions are raised: Is God unfair? Is God silent? Is God hidden? [Don Garner]

Yancey, Philip. *What Good Is God?: In Search of a Faith That Matters.* (Faith Words, 2010).
When belief in God is tested, does faith really make a difference? From ten experiences of sharing with believers in crisis–from the underground church in China, to terrorism survivors in India, to HIV/AIDS victims in South Africa, to traumatized students after the Virginia Tech shootings–the author bears witness to grace and comfort. [Don Garner]

Yancey, Philip. *Where Is God When It Hurts?: Comforting, Healing Guide for Coping With Tough Times.* (Zondervan, 2001).
The poignant question of "Why?" is common to many people touched by tragedy and loss. This award-winning and oft-reprinted book offers perspective on God which honors the feelings but seeks to lift the vision of persons who are suffering. [Don Garner]

CPSIA information can be obtained at www.ICGtesting.com
Printed in the USA
LVOW08s0437220114
370318LV00002B/7/P